Trains
[1001]
[photos]

© 2007 Rebo International b.v., Lisse, the Netherlands

www.rebo-publishers.com
info@rebo-publishers.com

Text: Françoise Huart and Ségolène Roy
Photography: Yves Lanceau and furrytails.nl
Co-ordination: Isabelle Raimond
Graphic design: Gwénaël Le Cossec
Original title: Les Chiens 1001 photos
© 2006 Copyright SA, 12, Villa de Loucine, 75014, Paris, France
Translation: First Edition Translations Ltd, Cambridge, UK
Typesetting: A. R. Garamond s.r.o., Prague, Czech Republic

ISBN : 978-90-366-2253-0

Trains
[1001] photos

REBO
PUBLISHERS

Contents

Full Steam Ahead!

Electricity Takes Charge

Diesel in Force

Organization and Networks

Railway Technology

Nostalgic Journeys

Railway Model Building

Full Steam
Ahead!

The first true locomotive was designed by Englishman Richard Trevithick (1771-1833), who presented it to the world in 1804. It used pressurized steam. This is when the history of railroads began. Although railways had already been known for a long time, their trucks were drawn by horses.

The appearance of the "locomotive" was a revolutionary invention in the field of traction. However, it was necessary to wait for another twenty-five years before the steam locomotive would be further developed. George Stephenson and his son Robert, who were also English, realized that this invention could be transformed into a fantastic tool for economic development. In 1825 they decided on a gauge of 4 feet 8 1/2 inches (1.435 m), the wheel gauge of road vehicles of that time. They tested one locomotive on the way from Stockton to Darlington, Great Britain, then constructed a machine and named it the "Rocket." It ran in 1829 for the first time and

won a competition in Rainhill. This new means of transport immediately gained the name "railway" because of the metal rails on which the vehicles moved.

The "Rocket" worked with technology developed by the French engineer Marc Seguin: it was equipped with a tubular boiler that supplied pressurized steam to a twin-cylinder engine which propeled wheels through a connecting rod – shaft system.

Fundamentally, the steam locomotive preserved these construction elements until

Railway Origins

it left production. A large number of technical improvements enhanced its efficiency, both in power and in combustion quality, making significant progress particularly with regard to speed.

[1] The reconstruction of the first German machine "Adler," is often presented in public.
[2] The Stephensons' "Rocket" (GB) as a part of a model-making exhibition organized in Cannes, France.

[3] One of the first Spanish locomotives, the 040 type, put into service by the company "Norte" (North).

22..ORLÉANS..LA GARE.CÔTÉ NORD

[4] The 220 "Jupiter" at Golden Spike National Historic Site (Utah) on the first transcontinental line. It is admired by the many tourists who visit.

[5] This British 030 forms part of the collection of engines on a tourist railway which succeeds in preserving the charm of trains of the past.

[6] A beautiful railway atmosphere at the end of the 19th century in Orléans (France).

[1] The "Pierrot" was designed in France in 1846. It has a type 111 axle configuration.
[2] PLM's 1423 locomotive (France), manufactured in 1854, may be seen in the Cité du Train (French Railway Museum) in Mulhouse.
[3] One of the first Swiss locomotives, named "Genf," (Geneva) is displayed in a conspicuous place in the Swiss Transport Museum in Lucerne.

[4] This "l'Union" locomotive, manufactured in 1897, was preserved by a French enthusiast. It comes from an industrial network.

[5] The evolution of forms is visible on this locomotive of the 030 type with a separate tender, operated by the "Compagnie de l'Est" (Eastern Company), France.

[6] A 030 type locomotive for hauling freight trains with its own separate tender. This one belongs to the Belgian state.

102 — Les Locomotives (Belgique)
Chemins de Fer de l'Etat Belge

Locomotive à 6 roues accouplées pour Trains de Marchandises
Construite par la Société de Constructions de la Meuse, à Liége

F ♣ F

[1] This is one of the oldest locomotives still in operation: the 671 of 1860 hauls historic trains for the Austrian GKB company in Styria.
[2] The locomotive prototype "Puffing Billy" is currently on display in the Museum of Transport in Munich (Germany).
[Right] Having been restored, the Belgian locomotive 18.051 is on display in a museum in Treignes, joined to the Three-Valley Railway.

[1] The locomotive 4.853 from1866, of the "Compagnie du Nord" (North Company), France, preserved by AJECTA.
[2] Designed by Hackworth, this No. 23 "Wilberforce" is one of the first British achievements.

"Lovett Eames." Single Bogie Express Locomotive. No. 5000.

[3] This American locomotive of the 211 configuration was named "Lovett Eames." It is an example of the type widely used at the beginning of railway transport on this continent.

[4] Designed in Germany, this 120 ran for the company Rheinische Eisenbahn until the end of the 19th century.
[5] One of the first German locomotives, "der Münchener," was designed by the company Krauss-Maffei, which became famous in the railway world.

[1] This 030 with its separate tender belongs to the Russian railways, and was manufactured for freight trains working on a Transcaucasia route.

[2] The No. 33 locomotive "Saint-Pierre," manufactured in 1843, is also part of a collection in the museum "La Cité du Train" in Mulhouse.

[3] Manufactured by the Cail company in 1853, the locomotive "la Carniole" was a 030 type with a tender.

[4] A 121 type with a separate tender, the Swedish locomotive "Gota," was put in operation in 1866.
[5] This passenger train of the "Compagnie du Nord" (France) is pulled by a 030 equipped with a tender.

Steam traction may be considered to have reached its peak in the 1930s, due to the increase in speed and power. The tremendous development of railways in Europe and consequently also on the American continent resulted in further demand for locomotive production.

In the 20th century, several renowned locomotive designers stepped into the market and, through technical innovation, developed locomotives which were more powerful, more reliable and consumed less energy. Despite being challenged by electric traction and diesel, steam traction remained omnipresent, though on a smaller scale. Various locomotive designers, such as André Chapelon, believed that their performance could be improved even further.

About thirty years later, research and construction of new machines gradually declined, as diesel traction came to be considered the traction of the future. In spite of that, certain Eastern countries continued to favor the older means of traction, although only for a short period of time. The oil crisis in 1973 generated a timid revival of research in the field of steam locomotives, especially in countries where coal was cheap and plentiful. Incidentally, the steam locomotive remained in operation in the USSR, Poland, East Germany, and China for at least twenty years after.

However, it is gradually fading away under the onslaught of diesel or electric traction, which started to reach their full expansion in the 1960s.

Rapid Progress

At present, the use of steam engines for commercial purposes is limited. In nearly two centuries of railway operation, the steam locomotive made an indelible imprint in the history. The surviving relics and the interest in them shown by enthusiasts testify to their rich history.

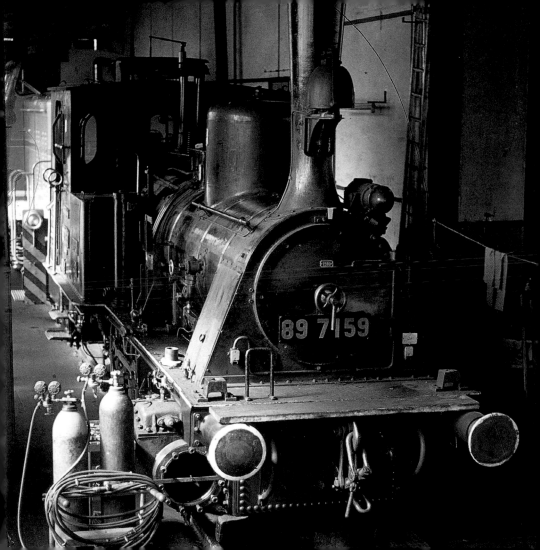

[1] A British train operating on main lines, headed by a 220 type locomotive of 1902, which belongs to the Midland Railway Company.
[2] Fuel loading in the "Pacific" locomotive in a depot in Calais under SNCF numbering. The locomotive started its career in the livery of the Northern Company (la Company du Nord) (France).

[3] An example of the "Pacific" locomotive at a metric gauge of 1.067 m (3.5 ft.), manufactured in India in 1949. This type was in active operation until the end of the 20th century.

[4] This British locomotive of American manufacture arrived in Europe with American forces in World War II. Today it is a part of the rolling stock of the Bluebell Railway tourist railway.

[1] The "Pacific" locomotive manufactured by the Baldwin Company in the USA in 1917 in the livery of the Frisco Lines Company.

[2] The Px 48 series of the 040 type with its separate tender was designed for a vast narrow-gauge Polish network. Some of the train units are still used at public events.

[3] In France the PLM Company also had "Pacific" steam locomotives at its disposal. This photo shows the 6102.

[4] The P 36 type locomotive (Russia) is one of the most successful designs from an aesthetic point of view. The series was developed at the beginning of the 1950s; however it has been fading out of use since the early 1980s.
[5] Steam traction was ephemeral in Switzerland. In 1902, the federal railways acquired the first units of the A 3/5 series.

[1] Introduced in Italy in 1907, the 130 locomotives of the 640 series remained in operation until the end of the 1970s. A few models are still employed pulling trains for enthusiasts. [2] Transformed and modernized by the PO Company (France) in 1937, the 231.726 remained the only locomotive of its type.

[3] This dual illustration shows the "Pacific" of the 231 H series operated by SNCF (France). This series is a result of the modernization of 85 locomotives which are used to pull express trains on main lines.

[4] A German locomotive of the P8 type put in operation by the Royal Railway of the Prussian Union in 1906. After being renovated, the 38.1772 occasionally provides traction for amateur or historic trains at film shoots.

[5] The fireman was in charge of supplying of coal in the firebox to maintain sufficient pressure.

[6] Possessing the necessary fuel, Poland developed several series of steam locomotives in the 1950s, from which the Ol 49 series derives.

[1] At full power, the "Pacific" of the Pm 3 type of the Polish railways pulls an express train composed of double-decker carriages.
[2] At an 0.76 m (2.49 ft.) gauge, the 031 T, type U No. 3, tows an excursion train on the Mayrhofen-Jenbach line in Tyrol (Austria).

[3] The 241 A 65, manufactured for the "Compagnie de l'Est" (France) in 1931, finished its career on the Eastern network of SNCF lines. After being purchased by a private individual, it was renovated in order to be put back into service in historic operations.

[4] Of metal and oil: detail of a beautiful connecting rod on one of SNCF's 140 C steam locomotives.

[5] An impressive steam locomotive of the "Garratt" type of the Spanish Railways is on display in Barcelona. It bears witness to the diversity of steam locomotives in the Spanish fleet.

[1] Steam traction was preserved in China until the end of the 20th century due to the abundance of coal. One of the last machines in operation is shown in the picture, moving a passenger train unit.

[2] In Jordan, the metric gauge Hedjaz railway uses partial steam traction, mainly to please the tourists and enthusiasts who come from all over the world to admire this type of locomotive. This example dates back to 1918.

[3] Detail of the finish of an impressive Chinese steam locomotive. The smooth operation of these steel giants was possible due to strict and regular maintenance.

[4] The Federal Republic of Germany (West Germany) terminated its regular steam traction service at the end of October, 1977. The illustration shows a machine of the 042 series shortly before the discontinuation of this mode of traction in West Germany.

[1] A 140 C leading a freight train in the east of France in 1975, in the year when the commercial use of steam traction was ended.

[2] A Portugal Railways metric-gauge locomotive of the "Mallet" type at the head of a short passenger train.

[3] With an 0.95 m (3.1 ft.) gauge, this 130 belonging to the Italian national company FS is about to pull a passenger train in Siciliana railway network.

[4] Two "Garratt" type locomotives passing in Zimbabwe at a gauge of 1.067 m (3.5 ft), jointed in more than generous dimensions. One of them is pulling a freight train as part of its regular operation.

By the beginning of the 1970s, steam traction had become a shadow of its former self. The vast majority of steam locomotives were taken out of operation after they completed their last railway tour, at the head of farewell trains.

This is often the last stop for a locomotive before it falls into the scrap merchants' hands. Some units, still in good condition, are sent to developing countries in trade. Nevertheless, the notion of railway heritage has just been born. The preservation of historic locomotives quickly arouses a lively interest.

A few wealthy individuals and volunteers join together into associations that strive to use all available means to prevent the destruction of locomotive types before it is too late. Associations were formed to save some secondary lines that were closed down as "unprofitable." To be able to operate these lines for tourist purposes, it is necessary to maintain the locomotives in working order. It is mainly those units that were saved from scrap that will run on the country railway lines reopened by enthusiasts.

At the end of the 1970s, around thirty tourist railways were opened in France, Germany, Austria and Great Britain, the country considered to be the birthplace of railways. Due to this activity, a significant stock of steam locomotives has been preserved. These days, they are often used for filming and historic reconstructions of all types.

Last Honors

Without such various events, only museums would commemorate railway history. At present, steam locomotives owned by associations or tourist railways are also experiencing a rebirth in countries outside Europe.

[1] Acquired for the German Democratic Republic (East Germany) shortly before the reunification of the two German states, the 52 8200 is a part of the fleet of railway traction vehicles in Three-Valleys, Belgium.

[2] Previously employed by the LMS company in Great Britain, the 5305 "Black Five" leads special trains.

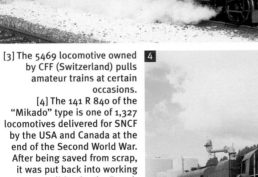

[3] The 5469 locomotive owned by CFF (Switzerland) pulls amateur trains at certain occasions.
[4] The 141 R 840 of the "Mikado" type is one of 1,327 locomotives delivered for SNCF by the USA and Canada at the end of the Second World War. After being saved from scrap, it was put back into working condition by the French association AAATV in Vierzon (France).

2 [1] The 230 G 353 was the last steam locomotive in the inventory of SNCF (France) to remain in active operation. It was used to haul special trains like this one in Paimpol (Brittany).

[2] This Polish locomotive of the 150 type, series Ty 2, of German origin, was preserved for leading amateur trains, and is also involved in film.

[3] With an axle configuration of 221, the 16.042 – a Belgian locomotive – forms a part of a railway equipment exhibition.
[4] The "Pacific" 231 K 8 – an old machine of SNCF (France) – is thr property of the MFPN association. It may be seen at the head of special trains or at steam traction festivals like here in Noyelles.

[1] This 130 with its separate tender 1367 is part of the historical heritage of Swiss Federal Railways (CFF). It pulls special trains upon request and may be seen at public events.
[2] This ex-Southern Railway British 030 T 1556 is owned by the tourist network KESR.

[3] Several Czech locomotives, the 498 106 among them, have been preserved and restored to such a condition as to be able to take part in public events or to pull special trains.
[Right] This 040 T, coming from an industrial network, runs for the Three-Valleys Railway (Belgium). It was named "André Chapelon."

[1] This well-preserved 040 T from a French industrial network was bought by a tourist railway established near Grenoble. The business line was closed later and all historical exploitation was prohibited.

[2] A 131 T of 1951 is waiting patiently in Volos (Greece) to be sent to a workshop and restored to a functional condition.

[3] The 141 R 420 was acquired by a French association in order to be put back into operation. It pulls special and historical trains and may be seen in various films.

[4] The Austrian 91.107 is standing in an engine depot near Vienna. After a few years of uncertainty it was renovated and returned to operation.

[5] The 040 T No. 384, owned by a German association based near Fribourg in Breisgau, was manufactured in 1927.

43

[1] This Waldenburgerbahn's (Switzerland) locomotive No 5, manufactured in 1902 with a gauge of 750 mm (2,46 ft), was renovated to haul historic trains.
[2] The French dynamic association AJECTA uses 140 C 231 to lead special or historical trains.

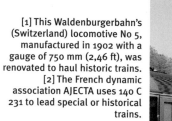

[3] Having immigrated to Belgium, 64 250 was running on a German network for a long time before it was returned to the Three-Valleys Railway. It was put back in working condition after several years in an engine depot and was repainted grey.

[4] For ex-Portuguese "Mallet," expatriation to Switzerland meant taking part in a steam festival at the bay of Somme (France). It is maintained and used by the Traction Association.

[5] It changed its network, but not its country. Ex-ÖBB 298 56 (Austria) of 1900 was acquired by the tourist railway Taurachbahn in Salzburg region.

3 [1] A British 030 T, named "Charwelton," is a part of the fleet of traction vehicles of the KESR tourist railway.
[2] Theis 52.1198 belongs to the ÖBB historical park (Austria) and pulls special trains departing from the capital.
[3] A Polish 150 of the Ty2 series seen during a celebration devoted to 150 years of railways in the country.

[4] A "Pacific État" preserved in France: the 231 G 558, formerly a SNCF machine and PVC property, was restored to a functional state.
[5] The 141 F 1111 is a Spanish historical locomotive which may be seen at various public events.
[6] Sold by ÖBB to the train charter company Brenner und Brenner, this 52.3879 pulled trains in Austria before leaving for the Netherlands.

47

S old as scrap, some trains are converted to "historic" machines, resold to associations or tourist railways, or displayed in museums transformed to monuments in public places.

This type of metamorphosis is most often seen in towns that have been strongly marked by railways in their history and still feature a large depot, a locomotive manufacturing plant, or the like. Train units may be placed in nurseries, in front of shopping centers, or they may become signs of restaurants or museums.

Where does the expression "flower pot" come from?

Transformed into an ornament, the locomotive bears certain similarities to a flower pot. Obviously, this is not a scientific term, but it derives from railway jargon, which is rich in juicy expressions.

These "flower pots" are "dead" machines, because various functional parts have been removed.

Generally, they are only repainted a "genuine" locomotive appearance, yet how many children like to think of becoming train drivers on board these inert machines?

Some locomotives have left workshops to be restored and put back into circulation, into life. In most cases, tourist railways discover the locomotives and carry out their refurbishment in order to enrich a fleet of traction vehicles which is often very limited. Nonetheless, many units, too damaged through lack of maintenance and lacking sufficient public interest, cannot be restored

"Flower Pots"

and end up one day under the torch of a scrap merchant.

[1] This ex-Zillertalbahn (Austria) 031 T with a gauge of 0.760 m (2.5 ft.) serves as a sign for a local museum in Jenbach (Tyrol). [2] A Spanish 130, photographed in Valence.

[3] At Reims train station (France), this C 313 is on display under a glass roof. In the past, this type of locomotive could be seen at the head of passenger or freight trains.

[4] Displayed on a pedestal, this cog railway steam locomotive No. 6 commemorates the early days of the railway line to Montenvers (France), and of steam traction.

[5] In Oslo, this No. 25 locomotive is on display at the central train station. This steam locomotive is a silent witness to the railway history of this country.

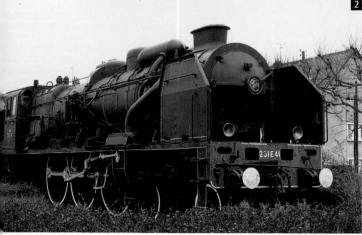

[2] [1] This Canadian Pacific 230 No. 1095 is on display in Kingston, Canada.
[2] Not far away from Tours, in Saint-Pierre-des-Corps (France), this ex-SNCF 231 E 41 is on display in a small public garden specially adapted for this purpose.

[3] This ex-ÖBB locomotive of the 95 series is on display in front of the Payerbach-Reichenau train station (Austria), the exterior of which is being renovated. Bad weather and vandals regularly damage these "flower pots."

[4] An ex-ÖBB, 031 T, is displayed in front of the train station in Mittersill (Austria). It is shown after the renovation of its exterior.

[5] This locomotive of German origin, numbered 5513 by CFL (Luxembourg), can be seen in Bettembourg in a public garden.

3 [1] On display in the park in the town of Engen (Germany), thise 64.520 of 1920 was purchased by a Bavarian museum and left its pedestal in 2004.

[2] This 41.195 steam locomotive is placed on a pedestal in front of a command post at the train station in Charleroi Sud (Belgium).

[3] This 021 T No. 601 of the Mexican national company N of M is on display in front of the Mexico City train station.

"Flower pots"

[4] A meter gauge locomotive is on display beside the sculpture erected in the memory of Marc Seguin, a great figure in the world of French railways.
[5] This ex-SNCF 140 C 287 is on display in the park of the Ferté Saint-Aubin castle near Orléans (France) alongside historic cars.
[6] This old shunting steam locomotive of the 030 type is placed on a small railway line section in San Diego (USA).

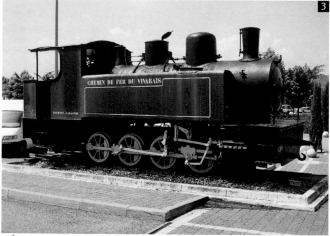

[1] This ex-Brittany "Mallet" E 415 has been preserved as a monument not far away from a station in Carhaix (France).

[2] This Bavarian 030 T (Germany) is on display at a school entrance.

[3] This 040 T has been placed in a supermarket parking lot, where it serves as an advertisement for the Vivarais railway, Mastrou.

[Right] Employed in the past as a construction locomotive, this 020 T is on display at the entrance to a service station near Lausanne in Switzerland.

ENTREPRISE
E.G.T.

LOCOMOTIVE ERBER, ST.
1899

Repos bien mérité
après la construction
des barrages du
St-Barthélemy, 1929-1931
C.D.C.

[1] This 040 T "Marguerite" is one of the engines preserved by the Mining Centre in Lewarde (France).

[2] A 240, a former RENFE (Spanish national company), locomotive can be admired near Madrid.

[3] A beautiful long "Mallet" locomotive may be seen in front of the headquarters of the Brazilian railway company RFFSA.

[4] A typical railway atmosphere near Mestre, Italy, with this locomotive coupled to an old passenger coach.
[5] A 131 T – from which various parts were removed – serves as a witness to the history of railways in Myanmar, formerly Burma.
[6] A 040 T, which originally ran on an industrial network and is now considered unsuitable, on a temporary rail before its placement in a supermarket parking lot near Lille (France).

Diesel in Force

A fter Great Britain, the next European railway lines emerged in France, Austria and Germany. In most cases they arose on the basis of private initiatives, because the state authorities remained mistrustful of technical projects.

A German, Rudolf Diesel (1858-1913), worked on a heat engine and registered his patent in 1893. However, his four-stroke locomotive was not completed until 1897. The internal combustion engine, later named the diesel engine, was not licensed right away. However, after 1910, various licences were granted for the navy, the aviation and car industries and...railways. The first large-scale implementation of the diesel locomotive was due to a military commission, World War I (1914-1918). As steam traction reached its peak, the competition in road transportation also picked up again. The railway companies woke up and ordered various diesel locomotive prototypes in ordered to streamline the exploitation of their lines.

The extinction of steam traction resulted in an increasing demand for diesel locomotives and their introduction in operation on main lines became widespread. In the USA, where diesel traction reigns practically without competition, the manufacturers produce powerful and reliable series, of which many exemples are manufactured under licence in France, Germany and Spain. This traction method is still used the world

An Explosive Invention

over, and it is the only mode of traction in certain African and South American countries. The diesel locomotive has experienced a certain revival as a railcar.

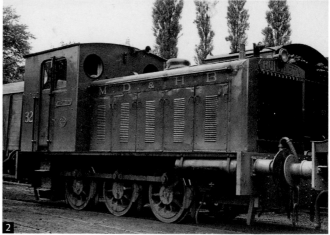

[1] This self-propelled wagon 2091.008, manufactured in the 1930s, was used in Austria until the end of the 1980s as a commuter train.

[2] This locomotive No. 32 was manufactured in Great Britain by Hunslet in 1932. It was preserved by a tourist network.

[3] This Hungarian railcar belonging to the Austro-Hungarian company GySEV was put into operation in 1926. It was in operation for more than 50 years.

[4] Used for shunting, the locomotives of the series A1A A1A 62000 operated by SNCF were of American design. The first locomotives were delivered in 1947. The series was declared unfit for service.

[5] A prototype of a diesel locomotive – V 32 01 – manufactured by Deutsche Reichsbahn Gesellschaft (Germany) in the 1930s. No other locomotives of this type were manufactured.

[6] Of British design, this French-made locomotive (BB 4036) was put into operation in 1946. It finished its career pulling construction trains in the employ of CFTA, a private French company.

[1] Manufactured according to a German-American design (Henschel/General Motors), the 2050 series operated by ÖBB (Austria) contributed to the decline of steam traction in its country. It pulled all types of trains, including main line trains.

[2] This railcar, manufactured by Wismar in Germany in 1936, was working in a local service on secondary lines before it became a part of a historic collection of the tourist railway.
[3] The locomotive V 36 231 was built in 1939, and is part of an important series of diesel locomotives supplied to DRG (Germany). Several units were saved.

[4] The BR (Great Britain) series 55 was known under the name "Deltic." It left its imprint in the history of diesel traction in its homeland.
[5] The Belgian series 46 railcars started working in 1952. This example was preserved in a functional state and is used as a historic machine.
[6] Diesel traction always remained small-scale in Switzerland. Nevertheless, since 1954, the CFF began receiving locomotives of the Bm 6/6 series, which are very useful for pulling maintenance trains along the electric lines.

[1] Dating back to 1939, this German railcar pulled school trains and was used at various special events on the 0.75 m gauge Möckmühl-Dörzbach line until the line's closure.
[2] With delivery starting in 1946, the standard gauge SNCB 62 series (Belgium) contributed to the elimination of steam traction in its country.
[Right] This railcar at a metric gauge, constructed by Michelin, operated in Madagascar.

[1] Made according to an American design and manufactured in the USA, this diesel locomotive works for the company NIR (Northern Ireland).

[2] A member of DB's family of V 200 locomotives (Germany), the 220.108 ended its career pulling amateur trains.

[3] A CC type locomotive developed according to a Swedish design and delivered to the Belgian Railways in 1955 is leading a freight train in Luxembourg.

[4] Of German origin, this Austrian shunter owned by the private company GKB was put into operation in 1938. Modernized and technically improved, it worked for a period of more than 50 years.
[5] A passenger train in Israel is pulled by two locomotives of the G 12 series of 1954. They were manufactured in the USA.

[1] The CFR's 80 series (Romania) has pulled light passenger trains and freight trains since 1966.
[2] This superb depot show of SNCF's CC 65500 locomotives (France) dating from 1955 can no longer be seen in Plaine. Some of them participated in the construction of new lines at various building sites.

[3] This German shunter worked in Switzerland for the Furka-Oberalp company. Despite its having being designed to operate on standard railway lines, it was adapted for the metric railway.

[4] As a part of DB's large V 100 family, introduced at the beginning of the 1960s, the 212.186 did hard work on the main and the secondary lines of the country.

In the 1930s, competition on the railways inexorably increased. The railway companies realized this and, feeling that their market share was declining, decided to react by modernizing their equipment.

In France, the private companies (SNCF was born in 1938 on the basis of the nationalization of railway companies) had faith in the expansion of diesel traction for pulling important trains that ran on the Paris-Lyon-Mediterranean transportation artery. They believed that speed was the key to competing with road and air transport.

The various attempts at improving the power-to-weight ratio of engines bore little fruit, and diesel locomotives capable of pulling heavy freight and passenger trains are rare on European railways. However, in the USA their role expanded much more quickly than in the rest of the world. In France, Germany, Spain, and Italy, the manufacturers of railway equipment finally received big orders for large series of internal-combustion locomotives at the beginning of the 1960s.

By the beginning of the 1970s, diesel traction had become ubiquitous. This wave lasted for only twenty years, and the diesel locomotive lines, whose development was interrupted, thereafter play only a secondary role.

However, they eventually enjoyed a revival of interest in regional railway lines. New machines are delivered not only to Europe,

Diesel's Expansion

but also to various American and Asian countries.

[1] In Spain, the RENFE disposes of heavy CC machines of the 321 series, which entered production in 1964.
[2] A "Eurorunner" type locomotive belonging to the locomotive rental company Siemens-Dispolok is pulling the private passenger train "Alex."
[3] The front part of an Iraqi commuter locomotive with 3,600 horsepower, manufactured in France.

[4] Several diesel locomotives are placed in a railway depot in Mossel Bay (South Africa).
[5] The 754 series owned by the Czech national company CD, produced by Škoda, appeared in 1979.
[6] A metric gauge B-BB locomotive of French designed is owned by the company Régie in l'Abidjan-Niger in Africa.

3

[1] Painted in the current colours of DB (Germany), this locomotive of the 218 series is a part of the V 160 family. The future of the series looks bleak.
[2] Inspired by America and operated by Slovenian railways, the 661 series is still of vital importance in everyday operation.
[3] The Argentinean network has powerful commuter diesel locomotives at its disposal, such as the unit in the picture.

[4] Two powerful Russian M 62s at the head of a freight train on the Finnish border. The gauge of 1.524 m is identical in both countries (5 ft.).
[5] Two Fret-SNCF BB 664000s parked in the engine house in Amiens (France). The second machine has been repainted in the current colours.
[6] At a metric gauge, this diesel locomotive pulls a passenger train in the Peloponnese network.

1] In addition to steam locomotives, the Chinese network received scheduled diesel locomotives like this exemple of the NY6 series.
[2] The ÖBB's 2016 series (Austria) is one of the "Eurorunner" locomotives of recent construction, which are manufactured in Germany. It is "universal."
[Right] A short passenger train is pulled by a 55 series locomotive from the Bulgarian company BDZ.

[1] An impressive Indonesian locomotive is pulling a short passenger train.
[2] Obtained by transforming an old Yugoslav locomotive, the 0.76 m (2.5 ft.) gauge D 10 of Zillertalbahn (Austria) pulls passenger trains.

[3] An exhibition of railway equipment in Warsaw (Poland), with a locomotive of the SU 46 series, the first part of which was delivered in 1974.
[4] The Greek national company has locomotives of a Hungarian design manufactured by Ganz-Mavag at its disposal.

[1] Shunting carried out by a DE 24 locomotive owned by Turkish railways. On a long-term basis, the American manufacturers were exporters, especially of diesel locomotives of all kinds. [2] In Australia, this commuter locomotive is working for the Queensland Rail company.

[3] Adapted from SNCF BB 67000 series, the BB 400 series of the company CFCO (Congo-Ocean), Africa, is composed of units running at a metric gauge.
[4] Diesel traction is also omnipresent in Egypt, although the country is equipped with engines of various origins. At a train station in Cairo, this locomotive of American origin is about to be linked to the head of a passenger train.

85

[1] A V 1500 series diesel
locomotive belonging to the
Austrian private company GKB.
It was put into operation
in 1973.
[2] In Africa, diesel traction
is essential, and it is provided
by machines such as this one,
operated by the national
company of Zambia.

[3] Operating on a track with a 0.95 m (3.1 ft.) gauge, this Sardinian diesel locomotive (Italy) is standing by the platform in Sassari on a line that is also equipped with standard gauge rails.
[4] In Great Britain, the British Railways company also modernized its fleet of traction vehicles by upgrading to diesel traction. In this picture, the 56 series machine is waiting for its next run.

In the diesel family, shunting locomotives occupy a special place. Genuine universal locomotives may be found at train stations or in classification yards. They may also be seen pulling short freight trains on secondary lines.

Although some designations in railway jargon may seem to have wandered far from their original meanings, "yo-yos" really deserve their name, because their work consists of incessant coming and going. In the past specialized, shunting locomotives took over various scheduled machine services, in particular on lines with weak transportation.

In certain countries, for example Turkey and Austria, they were even frequently seen pulling passenger trains. In other countries such as Switzerland, the "yo-yos" are not diesel machines, but specialized electric locomotives. This designation is no longer in use.

Removed from their previous service, the shunting machines and shunters have little chance to find a place in a museum. Some of them, sold to industrial concerns, are brought back to work on short distances. Others join tourist railways where they do the hard work practically identical to that which they previously performed. Finally, a few units obtained the status of "flower pot," but the machines selected to be thus displayed are not very numerous. Essential and widely used – certain European networks own a few hundred of them – the shunting machines are still a vital part of the railway scene. The reduction in the number

"Yo-yo" Missions

of trains pulled by locomotives for the benefit of railcars or electric railcars has led to a decline in this type of locomotive.

[1] This Greek shunter of German origin shunts in Thessaloniki (Salonica).
[2] An ÖBB (Austria) shunting locomotive in Vienna-South. This type of locomotive is also able to pull short goods trains.
[3] Shunting at a train station of Lamastre in Mastrou. This shunter is just about to take a passenger train to the railway platform.

[4]

[5]

[4] The size of some shunting locomotives is impressive, such as this 311 series locomotive in Spain. They are closer to locomotives than shunters.

[5] To be more visible at train stations, this Hungarian shunter which was developed in Budapest is provided with yellow and black stripes on its front.

[1] This German locomotive with a C axle configuration, owned by DB, is one of many train units delivered since 1955.

[2] At the Zermatt train station (Switzerland), a BVZ shunter is shunting an empty passenger train and taking it into an engine house for cleaning.

[3] At the depot in Tours-Saint-Pierre, a SNCF shunter is taking a scheduled machine placed on temporary boggles to a workshop.

[4] Tourist railways have shunting engines at their disposal as well. Bought second-hand in Germany, this shunter manufactured in 1963 does its work at a station in Mauterndorf (Austria).
[5] At a station in Sarrebruck (Germany) a DB shunter is switching an empty train and taking it to an empty depot. The use of electric railcars leads the reform of shunting locomotives in various European countries.

[1] Shunters were often used for pulling short freight trains, like this SNCF locomotive in Normandy (France).
[2] Freight wagons coupled to a passenger train at a station in Interlaken-Ost (Switzerland). A metric gauge diesel shunter belonging to the company BOB will lead the train.

[3] This type B shunting locomotive at an 0.76 m (2.5 ft.) gauge of the Zillertalbahn company is waiting for its next service run at Jenbach station. (Austria).

[4] Running at an 0.75 m (2.46 ft.) gauge, this locomotive of the German private company SWEG is provided with buffers for loading standard rail wagons onto carrier trucks.

[5] The T 466 series of the Czechoslovak company CSD was used as a shunting and a scheduled locomotive to pull short freight or passenger trains.

[1] An Italian shunter of the national company FS working at the Milan-Central train station.

[2] A service train is pulled by a 92 series Belgian shunter owned by SNCB.

[Right]
Shunters are also used to pull work trains, such as this locomotive photographed in the standard gauge BLS network in Switzerland.

[1] The SNCF's BB 63000 series was invariably used for shunting and pulling light freight trains. This specimen, removed from operation, was bought by the Three-Valleys Railway in Belgium where it was painted in...Swiss colors.

[2] A Finnish shunter of the Dv 15 series with a connecting rod, manufactured since 1962. Certain units of the series were modernized.

[3] The locomotives of the 2067 series, delivered since 1959 and equipped with connecting rods, carry out shunting at train stations, such as here at Vienna-West where they tow service and work trains.

[4] Several SNCF shunting locomotives are standing in a depot in Tours-Saint-Pierre (France).
[5] A DB (Germany) shunter of the 333 series put into operation in 1967 pulls a freight wagon. It was repainted blue and grey, which are incidentally also, by the way, the Rhine colors.

[1] Manufactured in 1934, this metric gauge shunter is equipped with connecting rods. It is part of the Provence (France) railway's fleet of traction vehicles.

[2] This Belgian shunting locomotive, also provided with connecting rods, belongs to the 73 series delivered for SNCB from 1965 onwards.

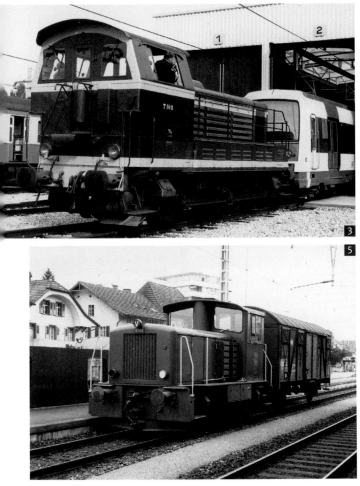

[3] This shunting locomotive with connecting rods, identical to the SNCF C 61000 series, belongs to RATP operating on Parisian lines alongside the French national company.
[4] With a gauge of 0.75 m (2.4 ft.), this Polish railways (PKP) shunter of the Lyd 1 type is widely used on the narrow-gauge railway networks.
[5] To serve clients without electrified branch lines, the CFF in Switzerland have heat traction shunting locomotives at their disposal, like this shunter of the Tm IV series.

Multiple examples of the
"Schienenbus" (bus on rails)
have been preserved as
historic vehicles.

n general, the name "Micheline" is used for a railcar operating on secondary countryside lines.

However this usage, although very common, is not correct. Its origin dates to the beginning of the 1930s. At that time, the company Michelin faced the problem of adapting pneumatic tires to the rail surface.

Modified railcars of this type have been manufactured since 1932 and may be thought of as buses on rails. They became known as "Michelines." These railcars, which were never very numerous, made it possible to avoid closing down some secondary lines where the operation of train units pulled by locomotives became too expensive. In earlier days, the networks were much larger than they are today, so it was thus inevitable that railway companies would reduce passenger service on the weaker transportation lines.

The railcar, which lost its place to the buses, experienced the same kind of rural expansion. Propelled by one or more combustion engines, railcars with one or two carriages appear in Europe in great numbers. German industry manufactured a one-carriage railcar type in a record period of time, a real bus on rails, which had both low purchase and maintenance costs.

In Eastern countries, another two-axle railcar model underwent an important development as well. We can say today that the railcar saved the lines from closure. The narrow gauge networks' rationalization also led to the acquisition of railcars in Europe. Several countries of South America remain loyal to the bus on rails to this day. They call them the "ferrobus." The development of

A Railcar Boom

regional links gave the railcar a serious nudge in the right direction and new series were then manufactured.

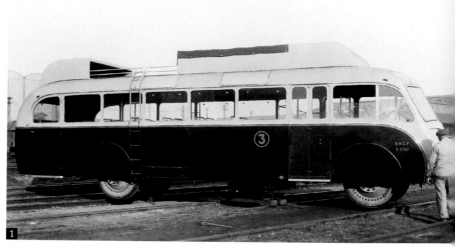

[1] A standard gauge bus on rails, Floirat, owned by SNCF. After it arrived at its destination, it was necessary to turn it around to be able to return. This requirement would prove the downfall of these locomotives. [2] Designed by the same manufacturer, these Floirat metric gauge railcars operated in Madagascar, generally coupled to towing units.

[3] One of three light two-axle railcars of the A2E type designed and manufactured in France in order to revitalize secondary lines. They have no successors, but ensure regular service in Brittany such as here in Paimpol.
[4] The CFL in Luxembourg obtained double railcars of German manufacture to carry out inter-city connections before the network's electrification.

[1] The Thai railway network also uses railcars of various origins on its main and secondary lines. [2] This 813 series double railcar is a part of the train stock delivered by Italian industry to the former Yugoslavia. It was integrated into the fleet of Slovenian railway traction vehicles when the country separated from Yugoslavia.

[3] West German railways commissioned this type of railcar in the mid-1980s for the purpose of rationalizing regional and local services. This is why it was produced in large quantities. A picture of this specimen was taken in Singen illustrating its original look, which was replaced later with a more visible bright red.
[4] Manufactured by Renault, there are not many SNCF's X 4200 series panoramic railcars - ten of them altogether. They enjoyed only a modest career before being retired.

[1] In Peru, a railcar of English origin manufactured by the Wickham company is part of the fleet of traction vehicles owned by the company FC Central.

[2] This French metric gauge railcar with its coupled towing unit was manufactured by the company De Dion. It is operating in Jordan.

[3] In the 1930s, the Eastern company in France was operating railcars manufactured by the Dietrich company.

[Right] Put into operation in 1954, this double Dutch railcar of the X-v series is leaving Aix-la-Chapelle (Germany).

[1] A double British railcar (BR) of the 158 series, seen in operation. The series was delivered shortly before the privatization of the railways.
[2] A new double railcar series, numbered 41, was put in operation by SNCB in Belgium at the end of the 1990s.

[3] The Finnish national company VR has been equipped with new one-carriage railcars of the Dm 12 series since 2004. They work on non-electrified regional lines.

[4] It was from 1987 that ÖBB, Austria, took delivery of the series VT 5047 mono-box. Their utilization on secondary lines turned out to be beneficial, but their limited capacity led to double operation in peak traffic hours.

[5] The DB (Germany) VT 641 series of French design is helping with the rational utilization of secondary lines.

[1] Two generations of German railcars side by side, with a MAN railcar coming from the 1950s, forming a reserve, and a "Regio Shuttle" manufactured by the Stadler company in 2004.

[2] A standard gauge single-carriage railcar of the Aln 772 series of the Sardinian (Italy) FS network. The 1940 series manufactured from the Fiat company remained in operation for a period of more than 40 years.

[3] The presentation of a prototype of the SA 121 series double motor railcar element at a train station in Warsaw (Poland) in the 1990s.
[4] The interior of this double motor railcar of the X 4500 series, seen at a train station in Arras, was modernized on the account of the TER service Picardy. The thoroughly modernised units obtained different front parts.
[5] Manufactured in France by the De Dietrich companies, this railcar of the ABK series was exported to Greece where it worked in the metric gauge network of the Peloponnese.

[1] The M 296.2 series single-carriage railcar, owned by the Czech company CSD, departing from the central station in Prague.
[2] A joint operation of a supplementary carriage and railcar on a 0.76 m (2.5 ft.) gauge line of Tamsweg-Murau-Unzmarkt, under the name Murtalbahn (Austria). This equipment was put in operation at the beginning of the 1980s.

[3] This "Ferrobus" of the Bolivian national company is running to the capital city, Sucre.
[4] Put in operation in 1942, this SNCB single-carriage railcar of the 49 series (Belgium) was bought by a local association to be put back in operation.

Electricity
Takes Charge

Research on electric traction for trains began well before the end of the 19th century. The intensive utilization of generators and permanent power units in industry led to electric traction in railways about fifty years after the beginning of the industrial use of electricity.

The first steps were halting. The appearance of a narrow gauge electric tractor manufactured by Siemens marked the beginning of electric traction. However, Europe was not alone in this discovery. In the USA, the Baltimore-Ohio Company also implemented its research results and consequently the Paris-Orléans Company in France took advantage of the American experience. The progress achieved in this area was great. In Germany starting in 1903, alternating three-phase current allowed for operation at 210.2 km/h (130 mph) for the first time, which was an absolute record for all traction modes.

16 Hertz 2/3 single-phase current systems were developed in Germany and Central Europe. However, at the beginning of the 1920s, individual companies often chose different currents, such as in France where a direct (continuous) current of 1,500 volts was developed faster than the single-phase current. Only after the Second World War did the 50 period single-phase current gradually replace direct current. Single-phase requires much less substantial infrastructure than continuous 1,500 volt current which needs heavy catenaries and many substations. Since then, the French lines

First Volts

have been supplied with this type of current, especially those lines which need to operate at a very high speed.

[1] Manufactured in 1924 for the Bavarian network (Germany), this EP series locomotive was preserved and is on display in a museum today.
[2] The first electric traction ran on the American B&O (Baltimore and Ohio) network. On the basis of conclusive testing, the French company Paris-Orléans decided to procure similar locomotives.

[3] In Switzerland, the company BLS opened its electric traction operation. This locomotive of the Be 5/7 series dates back to 1913.

[4] Having decided on electric traction early, the Swiss railway companies also procured locomotives adapted for working in mountain conditions, like this Saint-Gothard line. The series Be 4/6 of CFF was implemented from 1920 onwards.

[1] One of the oldest French electric locomotives hailing from the beginning of 20th century, the E 1 of the company Paris-Orléans, is a part of the collection of the Cité du Train in Mulhouse.

[2] This interesting engine on display in Munich (Germany) is regarded as the real first electric locomotive. It was developed by Werner von Siemens.

[3] A German electric locomotive of the E71 series put into operation in 1914.

[Right] An electric shunter from Switzerland owned by the Rhaetian Railway. It was manufactured in 1913 and due to its sturdiness, was able to remain in operation for more than 70 years.

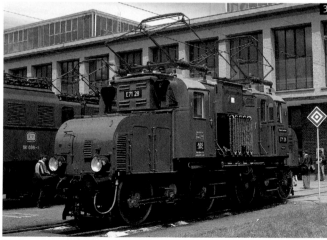

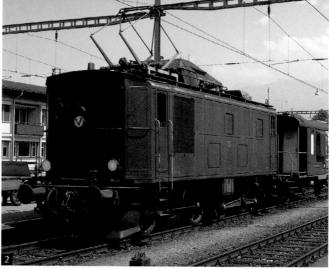

[1] This 2-axle electric railcar of a local Salzburg (Austria) railway began its operation in 1908. It ended its career as a service locomotive.

[2] This 313 locomotive belonging to the BLS company is shunting at Spiez train station (Switzerland). The machine was put into service in 1920 and remained in everyday operation for more than 60 years. During its career, the well-maintained locomotive was regularly refurbished in order to stay active.

[3] The E 244.31 of the BB type was put into operation by the DRG in Germany in 1936.

[4] In 1924, the Berne Montreux-Oberland (Switzerland) obtained this electric railcar with a baggage compartment.

[5] This suburban line from Innsbruck to Fulpmes (Austria) was one of the first electrified lines. This electric railcar, renovated, is from 1904, but the picture was taken nearly 70 years later.

[6] In 1929, the private German company Bayerische Zugspitzbahn obtained metric gauge electric locomotives with a B axle configuration.

[1] Bought second-hand by the private company Montafonerbahn (Austria), this 1045 is from 1927.
[2] A short passenger train belonging to the Swiss company EBT is pulled by a BB type locomotive of 1932.
[3] This metric gauge T9 electric locomotive hauled coal trains on the line Saint-Georges-de-Commiers-La-Mure (France) before it was transferred to the tourist industry.

[4] Delivered in 1930, this electric car of the Swiss company Rorschach-Heiden-Bahn ended its career as a reserve locomotive used during rush hours.
[5] A Rhaetian Railway (Switzerland) metric gauge locomotive of the Ge 6/6 I type, nicknamed "crocodile." The series was delivered in the 1920s.

[1] The 2D2.500 series by the company Paris-Orléans was delivered in the 1930s, and carried out its activities under the SNCF banner. It was subsequently renumbered as the 5500 series.

[2] This No. 11 locomotive was delivered in 1929 at the electrification of the metric time of the gauge line Viège-Zermatt in Switzerland. At the end of the 1990s it pulled supplementary or regular trains as a subsidiary locomotive.

[3] The BBB type E 626 series of Italian railways (FS) was put into operation in 1928 and worked for a long time.

[4]

[5]

[4] Another example of exemplary longevity is offered by this Ae 4/7 from CFF (Switzerland). Supplied from 1927 until 1934, the series remained in operation for more than 60 years. Several units have been preserved as historic vehicles.

[5] The DRG (Germany) E 18 series started its career in 1935. The last functional units were removed from operation in the mid-1980s, including this unit which is now displayed in Nuremberg.

E lectric traction was established in several European countries at the beginning of 20th century. In France, for example, the electrification of lines was initially implemented with a 650 volt third rail, as on the Paris-Invalides line in Issy-les-Moulineaux in 1900.

In Switzerland, electric locomotives have been operating between Seebach and Wettingen since 1904, while in Austria a local railway from Vienna to Baden was electrified in 1906, and the 0.76 m (2.5 ft.) gauge line in Mariazell was converted to electricity in 1909. Germany followed the movement, and the first part of the royal Prussian railways between Bitterfeld and Dessau was electrified in 1911. The 1920s were marked by an expansion of electric traction. Electric traction gained ground in Switzerland on the Berne-Lötschberg-Simplon line, as well as on the Rhaetian Railway, and likewise in Austria on the major transport artery of Arlberg, and also in other locations in Spain, Italy and Germany. In France, the year 1936 was eventful for the railways; electric traction appear in the Paris-Orléans company, in the Compagnie du Midi and on public network lines.

Although principally intended for trains running on main lines, electric locomotives do their shunting at train stations or in classification yards. Electric traction is developing equally in regional and inter-city services, in the form of electric railcars in

From the Beginning Until 1960

the former and tramways in the latter.

The underground, which of course operates mainly under the ground, benefits quite naturally from electric traction, enabling its development in all large cities of the world.

[1] Designed by Raymond Loewy, the GG 1 of the Pennsylvania Railroad company (USA) was a steel monster with a total weight of 219 metric tons. The illustration shows one machine restored to functional condition.
[2] At the end of 1940s the Ge 4/4 I series was delivered to Rhaetian Railway (Switzerland).

[3] A charter train of the Swiss company "Nostalgie Istanbul Orient-Express" several minutes before its departure from the Eastern train station in Paris. Its traction will be provided by one of SNCF's BB 16500 series.
[4] The E 636 series of FS (Italy) is composed of jointed locomotives with the BBB axle configuration commonly used in that country.

[1] As part of a series of machines supplied in the 1920s to the Austrian railways, this 1145 of the BB type will provide extra traction for a heavy freight train.

[2] A local passenger train composed of 2-axle carriages is pulled by a self-propelled wagon of the 4060 series manufactured in 1936, owned by ÖBB (Austria).

[3] A self-propelled De 6/6 electric wagon at a metric gauge on the Brünig line in Switzerland. It was put into operation in 1941. Several modified specimens serve as reserves even today.

[4] A special train chartered by a German travel agency is waiting at a train station in Merano (Italy) for its departure time to return home. Its traction will be supplied by a venerable E 636.

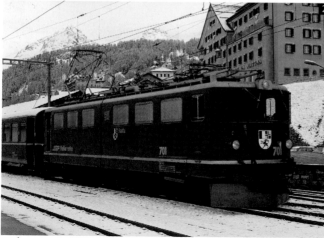

[1] Belgian locomotives of the 22 series were delivered from 1954 onwards. This unit, modernized and repainted in its company's current colors, was photographed in Brussels-Midi.

[2] The Rhaetian Railway (Switzerland) ordered Ge 6/6 II locomotives to reinforce the company's fleet of traction vehicles. The machines were delivered in 1958 (2 units) and 1965 (5 units).

[Right] The Italian E 645 series with BBB configuration is also composed of jointed machines like this locomotive photographed in Milan-Central. Their career is coming to an end.

[1] A work train in Norway is pulled by an El 11 locomotive hailing from 1959. This series is no longer on the list of working machines.

[2] Of French design and issued by the CC 7100 series owned by SNCF, this Spanish locomotive is inactive, and housed at a train station in Madrid. The Iberian version was delivered between 1956 and 1963. It is no longer a working machine.

[3] A railcar of the private company Stern & Hafferl is waiting for its departure time at a train station in Gmunden (Austria) equipped with three rails for metric and standard gauge trains.

[4] These locomotives earned the nickname "Waterman" because of their front parts which are reminiscent of the marks of ink-bottles. This unit is a part of 2D2 5500 owned by SNCF.

[1] Derived from the BB 8100 of SNCF, the 1100 series of NS (Netherlands) was delivered from 1950 until 1956. The picture shows a unit in its original condition. The series was later definitively removed from operation.

[2] The German E 10/110 series, delivered at the end of the 1950s, was primarily used on main lines. The operation of the series will be soon be terminated.

[3] A Swiss CFF electric shunter of the 1954 Tem II series, hard at work.

[4] Of German origin, this 1118 owned by ÖBB (Austria) is, in fact, a modified E 18. It provided for intensive transportation around Salzburg until the arrival of new machines.

[5] This SNCF BB series 12000 started its career on the lines of North-East of France in 1954. The series was put out of operation after 40 years of hard work.

[6] A regional train pulled by a BB 140 of DB stopping at a train station in Fribourg in Breisgau (Germany). The series, which was introduced at the end of the 1950s and as manufactured in large numbers, reached the end at its career hauling freight trains.

[1] This German E 94, after standing in front of the train station in Singen for a few years, was bought and renovated to pull freight trains.
[2] Belonging to the series E 428 III of FS (Italy), this locomotive of the 2BB2 type, which was put into service in 1939, is shown here pulling a heavy freight train.
This series was also declared unsuitable for operation.
[3] The Ae 6/6 of CFF started criss-crossing the Swiss network in the 1960s. The series, threatened at one time, still carries on its work, although less intensively than before.

[4] The CC 1020.042 is a historic machine from 1940, preserved in working condition by an Austrian association. This series hauled heavy freight and passenger trains for more than 50 years.
[5] A Re 4/4 I of CFF (Switzerland), repainted red after a general overhaul, is pulling a regional train on the Saint-Gothard line. It started working in 1946 and remained in service for nearly 50 years.

143

An E 14 series in South Africa,
acquired at the end
of the 1970s.

N etworks, the majority of which were nationalized, inherited locomotives manufactured or designed before the Second World War. The diverse rolling stock was not sufficient to meet ever-increasing transportation needs. Since heat traction was not developing any further and steam was on the decline, electric traction seemed to be an ideal solution.

Electric traction gradually took over the "elite" services such as TEE (Trans-Europe-Express), which were considered to be the jewels of the European railways at that time.
In the 1970s, freight transportation also took advantage of electric traction for the transportation of heavy trains loaded with minerals, iron and steel products or even, paradoxically, new automobiles. The idea of "universal" machines capable of pulling trains of all types was breaking through.

Those locomotives appeared principally in Germany, France, Switzerland and Austria. Power and speed were paramount, especially in France, Germany and Italy. Testing carried out with the machines manufactured in series showed that electric traction allowed for a high running speed. If the records from the 1950s served the publicity of large companies well, they also served the interests of manufacturers. The records justified important investments both on the national and international levels in order to

"Universal Locomotives"

provide "passengers" with the benefit of considerably reduced journey times. At the beginning of the 21st century, large series of locomotives are again being manufactured.

[1] Manufactured in a series issue of 10 between 1964 and 1970, the SNCF's CC 40100 left its imprint on the Paris-Brussels connection.
[2] This Japanese locomotive of the 2BBB2 type put into operation in the 1960s runs at a gauge of 1.067 m (3.5 ft.).
[3] This jointed E 656 of the BBB type, an Italian speciality, is moving at a Milan-Central train station to the head of a passenger train, which it will be pulling.

[4] Manufactured by Škoda from 1975 onwards, the 242 series is used by Czech Railways for all types of trains.
[5] The V 46 locomotive, also used for pulling short freight trains, is shunting at a train station in Budapest.

[1] Put into service starting in 1975, the BB 1044 series operated by ÖBB (Austria) hauls all types of trains.

[2] Combining beauty and dynamism, the CC 103 series operated by DB (Germany), which appeared in 1969, was the last word in German electric traction for more than 30 years.

[Right] The 91 series of BR (Great Britain) is composed of high speed locomotives equipped with only one driving cabin, and trains equipped with a subsidiary car on the opposite side.

[1] A BB 1142.5 of ÖBB (Austria). The reformed series was used from 1963 for the traction of all types of trains.

[2] A BB 25500, with a "grey concrete" finish, is about to pull a TER departing from Rennes. The series, which inaugurated its service in 1964, is in the process of being redesigned.
[3] The CFF in Switzerland obtained this 4 Re 4/4 IV in 1982. After taking care of the promotion of "Rail 2000," they were then sold to a private Swiss company.

[4] The Re 4/4 II of series of Switzerland served from 1964 until 1985. This machine is entering a train station in Lindau (Germany).
[5] SNCB in Belgium put the BB type of the 27 series into operation in 1981. It was intended for express passenger and freight trains.

[1] Working since 1974, the BB 111 series of DB (Germany) was principally intended for express passenger trains or regional trains. At present, these locomotives work only in regional transport.

[2] The 444 series of FS (Italy) of 1974 was modernized after 20 years of operation. It benefited from a modification of the body and streamlined front parts.

3 **4**

5

[3] The CFF (Switzerland) Re 4/4 II series – modernized and painted red – still remains a vital element in passenger transportation.

[4] The Swedish national company SJ has taken delivery of the Rc 4 series from 1970 onwards. It operates all types of trains of the BB type.

[5] The BB1163 series of ÖBB (Austria) entered service in 1994 as shunting locomotives and provided freight transportation. It was a part of the modernization of their fleet of traction vehicles.

[1] To modernize the rolling stock, the CFF (Switzerland) has been receiving vehicles of the Re 460 series of the BB type since 1992. It is used exclusively for passenger service in intercity trains.

[2] Developed and marketed in 1987, the 90 series of the British company BR was used to pull passenger and freight trains.
[3] The metric gauge Ge 4/4 II series of the Rhaetian Railway (Switzerland) was delivered in two stages: the first stage in 1974 and the second stage starting in 1984. Twenty-three units strong, this type covers a significant portion of the Rhaetian Railway's transportation needs, despite competition with more recent machines.

[4] A BB series 1116 named "Taurus" by ÖBB in Austria is pulling a regional train on a steep line in Tauern. This new generation began working in 2000.

[5] Painted "multiservice," this BB 16000 series belonging to SNCF (France) was put into operation in 1960. The renovation of these locomotives will be launched on a grand scale.

[1] Introduced in 1988 by the SNCF, the BB 26000 series called "Sybic," an abbreviation of words "synchronic and bicurrent", has been used for express, regional speed, and freight trains. The locomotive in the picture is shown it in its original livery, which is to be changed after a general overhaul.

[2] The EU 07 series of PKP (Poland) was put into operation in 1965. The picture shows a unit that underwent refurbishment and was repainted.

[3] Transport regionalization in Germany resulted in the acquisition of new equipment like this BB 146.1 series.
[4] In Australia, the 3913 locomotive hauls a passenger train belonging to the company Queensland Railways.
[5] With only one driving cabin, the series E 464 of FS/Trenitalia (Italy) has been used since 2000 in regional service and for trains on weak transportation lines.

157

Electric Railcars

The rational use of trains has always been a major priority. The electric railcar, which is more flexible than a classic train made up of a locomotive and carriages, elicited a positive response from both owners and passengers.

The first electric railcars appeared in the 1930s. The suburban networks around large cities can make best use of this type of equipment. It runs fast and is able to transport a large number of passengers. In Germany and Austria, railcars take responsibility for inter-city connections over long distances. Outside Europe, in Japan and in the former USSR, their utilisation is increasing. However, the limited number of passengers that may be transported, despite the train units being composed of three or four units, causes certain problems in the networks, as the potential passengers numbers are large.

A forgotten idea changed the situation in the middle of the 1970s with the construction of two-level trains. The transfer of this idea to the electric railcar brought it new vigor.

To cope with the development of the RER network in Paris, many double-decker railcars were put into operation. The circulation of trains was thus expedited, as this equipment was able to transport a greater number of passengers. Although large cities take greatest advantage of these railcars, single-level units have been developed in many countries of the world. They provide regional and sometimes also inter-regional connections.

Marginal in the past, the railcar has developed into an essential tool of railway transport. Increasing demand and the revival of regional and suburban services will allow the construction of new series.

[1] Bought second-hand by the Swiss company Oensingen-Balsthal Bahn, this electric railcar manufactured in 1935 ended its career after more than 60 years of service.
[2] A regional train was entrusted to an electric railcar of the 4030 series of ÖBB, manufactured in 1961. The series was later removed from operation.

[3] A SNCF Z 6100 railcar made of stainless steel in the northern outskirts of the capital of France. The series started its operation in 1965.
[4] Intended for RER-type trains in Paris, the Z 8800 series of double-decker electric railcars is bicurrent and has been available for delivery since 1987.

[1] Manufactured since 1949, the Italian Ale 840 series was in operation for 50 years before being removed from service. The last units were used as reserves as late as 2004.

[2] This electric railcar from 1913 was used by the Swiss company MOB as a reserve or supplementary locomotive.

[3] A Spanish electric railcar (RENFE) was manufactured since the beginning of the 1960s and intended for inter-city services. This one still appears in its original colours, and is just about to leave the capital.

[4] In the colours of BR (Great Britain), this 58 series unit was put into operation in the 1970s and runs between the outskirts and capital.

163

[1] The suburban lines around the Indonesian capital Jakarta are electrified and used by electric railcars.

[2] Nicknamed the "Break," the 300 series operated by SNCB since 1980 provides inter-city connections.

[3] Originally intended for express trains, this electric railcar of the ETR 220 series was manufactured at the end of the 1930s. It ended its working life as a charter train.

[Right] An electric railcar named the "Standard," which comes from the 1930s, gets its current by means of a lateral rail called the "third rail."

[1] Manufactured since 1987, the Aln 582 series of FS/Trenitalia provides regional and suburban connections.

[2] In Russia, a large electric railcar fleet is used for regional trains and also for medium-distance express trains.
[3] Composed of two "undeformable" elements with three boggles, the ET 426 series of DB Regio in Germany took over many regional trains.

[4] CFF put the RBe 4/4 series of 1959, which often used as a locomotive, into operation. After being renovated, they were allocated to support RER connections in Zurich.

[5] The national company RENFE (Spain) procured 3 element electric railcars of the 440 series in 1974. They were used for regional and suburban operation.

2 [1] An electric railcar of the ELD 4 series of NS (Netherlands) that provides inter-city connections is leaving the Amsterdam-Central train station. [2] Many Japanese private companies use electric railcars for operating on regional lines, such as this unit belonging to Keihin Electric Express Railway.

[3] Manufactured in Belgium and delivered in 1984, this Moroccan electric railcar may be seen at a train station in Rabat. It provides an inter-city connection.

[4] In South Korea, this railcar is about to leave Seoul on a fast service in the direction of a country town.

[1] The 70 series of the Norwegian Railways NSB was delivered in 1992. This equipment is used to service inter-city connections.

[2] At a large gauge of 1.626 m, this Portuguese four-element electric railcar made in1992 is working on a regional service line.

[Right] The "Z2" two-element series operated by SNCF, was released in several versions: express, bicurrent or regional. Here, a single-phase current unit, renovated and bearing the colours of TER, is leaving the train station in Tours.

[1] This three-element electric railcar of Polish construction, owned by the Slovenian company SZ, provides inter-city connections at medium distances.

[2] The Czech Škoda 470 series, which is composed of five elements of which three pull on two levels, was manufactured only in a single series of four and was put into operation in 1991.

[3] Belonging to the Italian private company FNM from Milan, this electric railcar – although renovated – dates back to 1928 and still runs as a subsidiary locomotive.
[4] Manufactured in 1913, this one-element electric railcar of the Swiss private company Aigle-Sépey-Diablerets remained in operation for more than 70 years due to its sturdiness, combined with a strictly observed maintenance program.

The front part of a train unit of
TGV Atlantique leaving
Alsthom workshops in Belfort.

Regular service at 200 km/h (124 mph) was inaugurated in Japan in 1964 with the "Shin Kansen" network, and began one year later in Germany. In France, the train "le Capitole" ran at this speed on adapted line sections in 1967.

The high-speed era began in 1981 with the TGV South-East reaching 150 mph. The same year, the 200 mph speed record of 1955 was surpassed by a TGV running at 228 mph.

The TGV Atlantique was opened in 1989, and in 1991 the SNCF beat the German record of 245 mph by reaching 310 mph. The North-European TGV was introduced two years later, and in Germany the "ICE" ran at a high speed from that time on. Italy began participating in the development in 1988, and Spain joined in 1992. The opening of the tunnel under la Manche in 1994 was a prelude to the circulation of the Cross-Channel TGV "Eurostar" between Paris/Brussels and London. In June 1996 the TGV "Thalys" started its service by joining Paris and Amsterdam, adding Cologne the following year. This was the beginning of a vast international network of high-speed trains. Several new lines were opened in Germany. At the same time, tilting trains reaching 120 mph or more ran in Sweden and Finland on classic adjusted lines. In Spain and Italy other new lines were built, while in France the European network will be completed when TGV East is put into operation (2007).

At Full Speed

In South Korea, the KTX connects the largest cities in the country, while in Japan the network "Shin Kansen" has made considerable progress. In the USA, the "Acela" trains have cautiously began their journeys. Russia and China are the countries to watch now. The operational speed of trains has increased up to 180 mph in ordinary service.

[1] In Germany, the DB has operated trains at 120 mph since 1965. They are pulled by powerful CC E 03 series.

[2] It is in Japan that the "Shin Kansen" concept of high-speed operation along with the creation of new rails was born in 1964.

[3] In Japan, the E 2 series of the "Shin Kansen" network, although single-level, allows the transport of 630 passengers at 165 mph.

[4] Having left Hendaye, this TGV Atlantique train unit is on the way to Paris-Montparnasse, its final station.

[2] [1] A TGV South-East train unit is approaching the French capital on a conventional line, as the new line has not yet been completed.

[2] In Japan, the pioneering country in very high speed train technology, equipment is increasingly aerodynamic, like this train unit from the 500 series of the "Shin Kansen" network.

[Right] The British inter-urban HST (high speed train) service started at the beginning of the 1970s as a diesel transport service.

[1] The success of high-speed connections in Spain made possible the construction of other lines so that the greater development of this system may be forseen.

[2] The SNCF train unit, holder of the world speed record of 310 mph, bears a plaque commemorating its technological achievement.
[3] Many towns in the southeast of France, as here Aix-les-Bains, have become "TGV stations."

[4] Designed by Ettore Bugatti, this diesel railcar owned by the State company (France) opened a high speed line in the 1930s.
[5] It was in 1992 that the first Spanish high-speed AVE trains started operating between Madrid and Séville.
[6] Running at 180 mph, this TGV Atlantique train unit is running alongside the A 10 motorway approaching Paris-Montparnasse.

[1] The first Italian high-speed trains, the ETR 450 series, were tilting trains allowed to operate at increased speed on a convectional line.

1

2

3

[2] The ETR 500 series of Italian high speed trains, which can reach 180 mph, does not tilt.
[3] At the bottom of Mount Fuji in Japan, an electric railcar of the "Shin Kansen" high speed network.

182

[4] The first generation ICE train units were put in operation by ICE in Germany in 1991.
[5] An encounter of 3 machines (Italy, France and Germany) at the time of a high-speed congress held in Brussels.
[6] A view of the interior of a first class coach of a first generation ICE train unit.

[2] [1] Thanks to the tunnel opened under the English Channel, "Eurostar" service high-speed trains operate between Paris, Brussels and London.
[2] Detail of the front part of a double-decker "Duplex" TGV carriage operated by SNCF. Over the course of years the form has become round.
[Right] A "Thalys" train unit heading for Cologne at its departure from Paris-North. These connections are supplied with special quadricurrent equipment.

[1] Running at 180 mph, a TGV "Eurostar" is borrowing a high-speed line from North-European TGV.
[2] In the USA, high speed made its first timid steps in 2000 with the "Acela" trains.

[3] Connecting Stuttgart and Zurich, a ICE-T tilting train unit of the national company DB approaches a station in Singen, Germany.
[4] Coming from Paris-North, this TGV "Thalys" has just arrived at the Amsterdam-Central station.

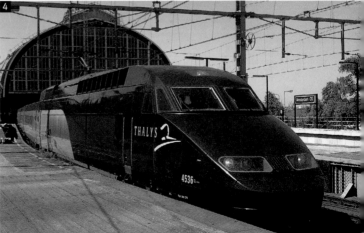

[1] The AVE train unit in operation on the new line Madrid-Lérida-Barcelona. The search for dynamic solutions results in interesting forms.
[2] The KTX, a high speed Korean train unit, has a form reminiscent of the French TGV.

[3] The front part of the power unit of a "Duplex" type high-speed train at the Paris-East train station, the origin of the East European TGV.
[4] "Alaris"-type Spanish tilting train units may be operated on conventional rails at a very high speed.

Organization
and Networks

Railway history is a process of constant renewal. As private corporations that were often very rich and powerful, nearly all railway companies were at one time nationalized to protect the notion of "public transport." Today, the phenomenon is reversing: they are being privatized.

At the dawn of railway development, the authorities showed little interest in the utilization of railway lines. The railways were developed with the aid of private capital, which was accompanied by the creation of a multitude of companies of various sizes, owned by manufacturers, bankers, and rich mine owners. However, this multiplicity caused problems. To travel from Paris to Vienna at the beginning of 20th century, a train had to run on the lines of approximately fifteen companies. The competition and sometimes poor management forced various governments to support these railway companies financially, and the presence of deficits pleased railway opponents. Nationalization was the generally proposed answer. It was effected in Germany and then in France, before impacting the vast majority of European networks. Important companies disappeared, to the great displeasure of shareholders, who were offered only meagre compensation.

Although the "private" companies never completely disappeared, from the end of the 1990s they experienced a resurgence in

National or Private?

connection with the liberalism recommended by European institutions. Generally acting on a local or regional scale or in the field of freight, they play a complemenary role to the national enterprises. The inverse process of privatization of large enterprises began in Great Britain; however, the network was poorly prepared and distributed with little judgment.

[1] In Grisons, Switzerland, the Rhaetian Railway has a vast metric gauge network at its disposal.

[2] This Belgian locomotive is rented by the Dutch private company Lovers Rail.

[3] The initials of the Swiss national company are written in three languages: SBB-CFF-FFS.

[4] A double railcar of the
Slovenian national railways
SZ is entering the station in
Ljubljana.
[5] A second-hand motor railcar
of the private Austrian company
Montafonerbahn on the
Bludenz-Schruns line.
[6] A diesel motor railcar of the
HST trains used by the national
company British Railways.
It has since been replaced
by thirty private companies.

[1] A 319.3 series diesel locomotive belonging to the national Spanish company RENFE.

[2] The NdeM logo belongs to the Mexican national company.

[3] This BB 111 series belongs to the German national company, at that time named Deutsche Bundesbahn (DB).

[Right] A BB 15000 series operated by SNCF.

[1] Amtrak, the American national company established at the beginning of the 1970s, is in charge of passenger rail transport for the whole country. It operates long- and mid-distance night trains.

[2] With a 0.76 m (2.5 ft.) gauge, this diesel locomotive belongs to the regional company Railways of Styria in Austria and operates on the line of Murtalbahn.
[3] Two diesel locomotives of the national company of Zimbabwe, NZR.

[4] Two railcars flank a trailer at the departure hall of Edolo in Italy. This equipment belongs to the private company Ferrovie Nord Milano (FNM).
[5] Photographed in North Paris, this locomotive of the 15 series is part of the rolling stock of the national company SNCB (Belgium).

[1] The Swiss private company BLS Lötschbergbahn is an active partner of the Helvetian network.

[2] Several private operators regained their place in the network after the privatization of British Railways, like the Connex company.

[3] The German DB split into several independent entities that secure regional transport, such as DB Regio, which owns this 143 series locomotive.

[4] Shuttle trains operating
in the tunnel under the English
Channel are operated by the
Eurotunnel company.
[5] Passenger transport
in Canada is in the hands
of the national company
VIA Rail.

[1] The division of SNCF into self-governing companies resulted in the formation of Fret SNCF. A diesel train is crossing the Nogent-le-Rotrou train station in Eure-et-Loir.

[2] Bought second-hand, this ex-DB BB 212 series is running under the German private operator Nordbayerische Eisenbahn.
[3] A regional connection in Germany is entrusted to a Swiss railcar owned by the private company Mittelthurgaubahn.
[Right] One of the newest TER Centre railcars. The regional transport, named TER, is used by the Regional Action for SNCF.

[1] An electric locomotive of the Hungarian national company MAV.
[2] A private passenger train in Germany, operated under the nickname "Alex" (Allgäu Express), a partnership between the German company Die Länderbahn and the Swiss company EuroThurbo.
[3] This BBB metric gauge diesel is owned by the Bolivian national company.

[4] The CFF Fret division in Switzerland is called Cargo CFF; since transport liberalisation, this BB series 421 has been running regularly in Germany.
[5] Manufactured in France, this powerful CC was put into operation by the Iraqi national company.
[6] A BB type "Taurus" of ÖBB at a connecting station in Unzmarkt. It is a part of the rolling stock of the Austrian national company.

The metric gauge line
from Saint-Gervais to
Vallorcine is one of the most
beautiful lines in France.

In contrast with the main lines that provide for national and international transport, the function of secondary lines is regional or local. Often used by private enterprises, these lines are usually short and their infrastructure is simplified.

Whether the secondary lines operate on standard or narrow gauge lines, their starting stations are located at important train stations situated on main lines. In general, they provide connections with trains operating on the main lines.

Railcars or self-propelled wagons wait for passengers and then take them to their destinations. Although secondary lines are rarely electrified, electric secondary lines may be found in Switzerland where the aerial line is omnipresent.

Certain lines where passenger transport has declined now only handle freight transport at a frequency of one train per week or every few days, according to transport along the line or at the end.

The revitalization of regional transport in Europe as well as in the USA has rejuvenated various secondary lines. Marginalized, the small lines had little future, but increasing consciousness of certain factors such as rural depopulation and the battle against pollution has reopened the old discussion about a role for secondary railways. After years of inaction, various countries have decided to implement new policies consisting in the transfer of their respective competences to third parties, private firms or local enterprises. An

Secondary Lines

economic revival at the European level enables many lines to be restored to operation after having been renovated and modernized.

[1] An example of a lost "secondary," the metric gauge CFD Lozère at a train station in Sainte-Cécile d'Andorge. One of the last railcars may be seen departing on the right side of the illustration.

[2] This one also has not survived. This standard gauge line near Saint-Dié (France) was finally closed in the 1970s, due to lack of investment and renovation.

[3] The privatization of narrow-gauge Polish lines resulted in closures and conversion into tourist lines.
[4] In the past, the famous Mont Saint-Michel was served by narrow gauge trains. The service has been out of operation for only a short period of time.

Côte d'Emeraude   113. MONT SAINT-MICHEL — Départ du Tramway (2)

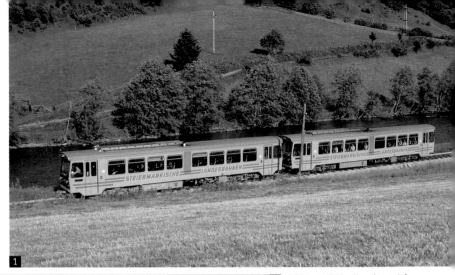

[1] Murtalbahn line (Austria) at a 0.76 m gauge. Its modernization made it possible to avoid closure.
[2] In Austria again, but at a 1 m gauge, this regular passenger train runs between Gmunden and Vorchdorf. The carriages are not new and their replacement is inevitable in the near future.

[3] A secondary line operated by Die Bahn in Germany.
[4] A standard gauge railcar owned by the German private company WEG on the Amstetten-Gerstetten line. Low traffic frequency led to its closure and later reopening by a rail association.
[5] A 0.76 m (2.5 ft.) gauge line in the Rhodope Mountains, Bulgaria, where freight transport ended. Only passenger transport remains.

[1] Certain private companies still transport freight, like here on the Breisach-Riegel line run by the SWEG in Bade-Wurtemberg.

[2] The train station in Lumbres (France) is a departure point for the tourist railway of the Aa valley.

[3] In Sardinia, a 0.95 m gauge line network still exists. Some of the lines are operated only in the summer for tourists.

[Right] Operated in the past by the German Democratic Republic's company DR, the metric gauge network of Harz was privatized in 1993.

[1] Too few passengers on the standard gauge line between Gaildorf and Untergroningen in Germany resulted in the termination of passenger transport on that line. Freight trains are still in service.

[2] Around Valencia (Spain), a secondary line network operated by the company FGV takes care of suburban train service.

[3] From a vast network operating in the department of Mamers-Saint-Calais in Sarthe (France), only the Beillé-Bonnetable line has remained in operation as a tourist railway.

[4] The 0.76 m (2.5 ft.) gauge Jenbach-Mayrhofen line (Austria) was modernized using new equipment. A regular passenger railcar service also accommodates hikers and tourists.
[5] Only a few lines of a vast metric gauge network in Portugal have remained in operation for tourists, like the one in this picture leaving from Porto.
[6] The only CFF metric gauge line in Switzerland, the Brünig line, merged with the private LSE company in order to create a new Zentralbahn entity, allowing for more rational and efficient operation.

[1] The metric gauge Breton Network was truncated; however, two lines survived after their conversion to standard gauge. These lines run from Guingamp to Carhaix and to Paimpol, and they were integrated in the TER Brittany network.

[2] In France, the Cerdagne line – also as known "Canari" – is a mountain railway electrified by a third side rail. It operates between Villefranche-de-Conflent and Latour-de-Carol.

[3] Reduced to only occasional service, the BA (Blanc-Argent) metric gauge network provides TER services for the central region between Salbris and Luçay-le-Mâle (France).
[4] In Greece, the important Peloponnese metric gauge network was modernized and rationalized. Long-haul direct trains run there.

[1] The Liestal-Waldenburg (Switzerland) line at a 0.75 m (2.5 ft.) gauge is a modern regional railway near Basel.

[2] A metric gauge train of the Swiss private company Bière-Apples-Morges is carrying freight carriages on standard gauge carrier wagons.
[3] The German private company Railways of Hohenzollern uses a standard gauge line network, both for passenger and freight transport.

[4] At the Bastia train station (Corse/France), a freight train is getting ready to depart in the direction of Ajaccio.
[5] In Italy, the Tramway in Renon near Bolzano uses tram-style electric railcars.

A vast forest network
operated in Romania
ten years ago.

T he railway formed an integral part of the industrial revolution of the 19th century. Nothing could be more natural, for it too would be developed within factories and industrial and mining complexes. The railway became a tool permitting the expedition of production and the delivery of raw materials.

To enable large industrial companies to transport wood, coal, iron ore and metals, important railroad networks were built in Europe as well as outside the old continent. Industrial networks employed hundreds of locomotives and thousands of wagons. In various countries with large industrial production such as the former USSR, China, the USA, Germany and France, these networks became vast, requiring the use of many locomotives and thousands of wagons specific to the type of transport.

Dependent on both national and world economies, various well-established groupings experienced closures and abandonment of sites. Roadways proved to be fierce competition in this field.

At the same time forest networks – usually at a narrow gauge – completely disappeared from Western Europe, while in Romania and Hungary several rare lines are still utilized and have survived thanks to tourists.

Several sugar networks are still active in Indonesia. As a rule, secondary lines are short side lines serving factories or warehouses. Usually they are worked by

At the Service of Industry

shunters, which are often acquired secondhand. Track and network maintenance companies also appear in this area.

[1] The staff of the military
base in Pruniers (France) travel
to the site by train.
[2] A SNCF branch, the VFLI
(Voies ferrées locales et
industrielles) company, uses
various industrial networks
and branch lines.
[3] The industrial railway
Endorra-Escatron (Spain) had
impressive railway equipment at
its disposal for transporting ore.

[4] On the Island of Java, Indonesia, the production of sugar cane was conveyed by a developed industrial network using venerable steam locomotives.
[5] The quarries of Saint-Nabor in Alsace were dispatching their production in wagons on an industrial line connected to the SNCF network.

[1] An industrial complex in Basel has a network of side lines served by diesel shunters.

[2] Two diesel locomotives are shuttling at a power station in Brazil.
[3] The sugar house in Boigny has brightly-coloured shunters at its disposal to return the Fret SNCF loaded wagons.

[4] Specializing In the production and maintenance of work locomotives, the Matisa company joined the SNCF network.
[5] The Mure Railway in Dauphiné (France) used to work as a mining network; it was transformed into a tourist railway after the mine closure.

[1] A good example of a factory junction. This shunter is pulling wagons dispatched by the SNCF back to its client in the South-East of the country.

[2] Factory shunters represent a not insignificant portion of the market. This picture illustrates a locomotive produced by Krauss Maffei in Germany.

[3] Located in the outskirts of Paris, the industrial railway of Aubervilliers used to serve a vast industrial network.
[4] In Romania, the forest lines are still in operation, and they also transport tourists on request.
[5] The 0.60 m (2.0 ft.) gauge sugar network in Pithiviers was closed for all transport, but a short line continues operation as a tourist railway.

[1] In South Africa, the output of a coal-mining complex is dispatched by railway.
[2] The Alsdorf mines in Germany operated a vast industrial network until the closure of the site.
[Right] The mining railway Pontferra-Villablino in Spain utilized steam locomotives for many years.

[1] Purchased second-hand from DB in Germany, this diesel locomotive is pulling a work train as part of a line renovation project in France.

[2] The forest network in Abreschviller (France) ended its operations, but part of the line was preserved as a tourist railway.

[3] In Germany, the industrial Dortmunder Eisenbahn network is vast and complex. Powerful diesel locomotives haul heavy freight trains.

[4] The Mines Network in Blanzy (France) was a large, electrified network. Several BB type electric locomotives provided transportation in the mines.
[5] Another example of a factory using a train to transport loaded carriages to the depot. There they will be coupled to a train operated by SNCF.

[1] This ex-DB (Germany) diesel locomotive is used by Pivato, an Italian company that provides railway maintenance.
[2] Second-hand equipment is acquired by construction and maintenance companies. An ex-SNCF locomotive forms part of the rolling stock of the company Travaux du Sud-Ouest.

[3] Iron ore extracted in Narvik (Norway) is transported by railway. Heavy but powerful locomotives are necessary for this type of transportation.
[4] Tunnel cutting is accompanied by the laying down of working rails. These are served by diesel shunters authorised for this type of work.

A t the beginning of the 20th century, railway companies reorganized their passenger services by creating train categories, and the first direct train operated in Germany. The concept of main line and slow trains appeared only at the beginning of the 20th century.

It was the beginning of the separation of services offered to passengers: local, national and international.

The main line trains are considered "elite" trains that offer the benefits of the finest trappings and attentive care for a clientele that demands speed, comfort and perfect service. The "fast" trains are successors to the "speed trains" put into operation by the Compagnie du Nord in France. They were soon joined by "express" trains which are generally distinguished by making more stops than the "fast" trains. Luxurious national and international trains, a large number of night trains, and several classic day trains became the standard bearers of their companies in both Europe and the American continent. Consequently, the torch in Europe was passed to TEE trains.

The creation of a high-speed line network has had an impact. The number of fast trains and express trains has declined, which was beneficial to TGV in France, ICE in Germany, and AVE in Spain.

First launched in Germany, the interregional trains are in fact express trains that operate over short distances. They were further

Rapid and Express

developed in Switzerland and Italy. In France, the TER are regional express trains, but most of the time they still stop at many stations.

Rail Motor. L. B. & S. C, Ry.
West Croydon & Epsom Downs.

[1] At the beginning of the 20th century, a British company near West Croydon used shuttle trains with steam locomotives in the middle.
[2] A picture of an express train from the 1930s in Germany, pulled by a powerful DRG "Pacific" 01 series.

[3] An express train of the
Compagnie du Nord
in France pulled by an elegant
230 type steam locomotive.
[4] In Peru, this railcar departing
from Huancavelica is making
a connection.

BORDEAUX - Gare du Midi (*Le Hall*)

2 [1] Pulled by a heavy electric GG 1 type locomotive, this is an express passenger train of a company from New Jersey. [2] Monumental train stations were built in response to railway development, such as this one in Bordeaux, seen at the beginning of the 20th century.

[3] In South Africa, the "Orange Express" train with steam traction is covering the Durban-Cape Town connection.
[4] An SNCF express train at the end of the 1960s. A CC series 7100 is pulling the train.

[1] In Great Britain, the HST type fast trains started with diesel traction.

[2] Originating in the Belgian capital Brussels, SNCF's CC 40100 is pulling a fast Corail train to Paris.

[3] A Swiss domestic intercity type train shown departing from Brig, pulled by a BLS machine.

[Right] Streamlined to gain speed, this "Pacific" type steam engine is pulling an express train belonging to the American Baltimore-Ohio company.

[1] An accelerated MOB passenger train is just about to leave Montreux for the destination of Zweisimmen (Switzerland).
[2] Automobile trailer cars – porteautos – are placed behind the Bregenz-Vienne locomotive of Arlberg.
[3] In the past, journeys were more comfortable, as is shown in this picture of the interior of the first class coach belonging to the company Paris-Orléans (PO).

[4] A "Metroliner" express train belonging to the Amtrak company, operating in the Washington-Boston corridor.
[5] A reception for the staff of DSB inter-city trains in Denmark.
[6] The SNCF express train "Corail Téoz" travelling near Saverne (France) on its way to Paris.

[1] The interregional train Brennero-Bologne (Italy) is composed of renovated parts and painted in the colours of FS/Trenitalia.

[2] A SNCB train of the InterCity category at the departure area of Brussels-Midi. It is composed of air-conditioned electric railcars of recent manufacture.

[3] An express train of the Czech CD company at the departure area in Mariánské Lázne.

[4] A DB (Germany) InterCity express train stopped at Prien station (Bavaria) on its way to Berchtesgaden.
[5] An express train of the Finnish VR is pulled by a Dr 13 series diesel locomotive derived from the SNCF's CC 72000 series.
[6] A Geneva-Milan international express train near Aigle on the Simplon line. The first coaches run beyond Brig to the Lombard capital.

It is necessary to state openly that long-distance train journeys and railway adventure belong to bygone times. There was and still is aviation. There are also high speed trains now, which have contributed to the decline of classic trains, it's true, but also to preserving railway transport.

Established in 1957, the Trans-Euro-Express (TEE) network offered first-class express trains with catering, intended especially for business clients.

A vast European network based on high-quality services and speed took its place a few years ago. However, the considerable success of this type of train must be considered in the light of its lack of second-class coaches.

The strong demand for fast international trains with two classes rang the death knell for the last TEE trains, which were replaced by "EuroCity" (EC) trains after 1987. Formed by a homogenous train unit, the first-class coaches are separated from the second-class carriages by a dining or buffet car. The EC trains have experienced increasing success. The employment of comfortable new air-conditioned coaches has ensured the popularity of the service, which does not neglect to engage in marketing activities with its captive clientele. The opening up of former Iron Curtain countries has allowed for the creation of new East-West links in the 1990s.

The development of new high-speed connections necessarily reduces the number of conventional trains.

Across Europe

The EC is not exempted from this rule, and conventional trains are gradually being reduced on many of the important international lines, to the benefit of, for example, TGV and German ICE train units. According to current predictions, Eurocity trains may survive for another few years, but they will have to abandon their place to the newcomers.

[1] An Italian railcar provided the TEE "Ligure" connection between Avignon and Milan via Nice, and it is an IC International with two passenger classes took over its route in 1982.
[2] Interior of the domestic TEE known as "the Mistral," which used to be one of the most renowned trains in France. It ran between Paris and Nice and lost its place due to the expansion of high-speed trains.

[3] An electric railcar of the Dutch company NS is waiting at a station for its departure. It will be running as the TEE "North Star" between Paris North and Amsterdam.

[4] The success of the TEE "Mediolanum" on the Munich-Milan route resulted in the replacement of motor railcars by a towed train unit.
It was replaced in May 1979 by a train composed of coaches with two classes.

[1] The route plaque of the TEE "Île de France" was nicknamed the "cinéma" by railwaymen as it was illuminated.

[2] The TEE "Gottardo" provided a Milan-Zurich connection via the Saint-Gothard line.

[3] The TEE "Capitole" (Paris-Toulouse) ran at 120 mph on a part of an adjusted line, thus gaining it popularity among clients.

[4] Pulled by a quadricurrent CC of the SNCF 21000 series, the TEE "Cisalpin" is approaching the Swiss border, where the train will be taken over by a CFF machine.

[5] The TEE "Cisalpin" begins its journey from Paris to Milan. The air-conditioned coaches and dining car provide a comfortable journey. It was replaced by a TGV link between Paris and Lausanne.

[1] The SNCF train unit "Grand Confort" at the Orleans station for a special event. This type of equipment ran in TEE service, in particular to Paris-Toulouse. A buffet car is in the front.
[2] The interior of a "Grand Comfort" coach after its renovation for use in fast trains between Paris-Strasbourg.
The picture shows its catering service.

[3] Running between Geneva and Milan, the TEE "Lemano" was composed of Italian coaches. Its traction was generally provided by a Swiss unit, by the CFF machines painted in TEE colours.
[4] A stainless steel SNCF dining car. The sleeping carriages team provide catering services and offer sophisticated, high-quality meals.

[1] In 1977, 500 "Eurofima" cars bearing the name of the organization financing the operation were put in operation on fast international lines. The train in the picture works for Italian Railways.

[2] At a Basel station, this Eurocity train is about to leave for its destination of Amsterdam. It is composed of Swiss carriages.
[3] Danish IC3 train units of the national company DSB are working the Eurocity connection between Copenhagen and Hamburg.

[4] The international train "Transalpin" (Basel-Vienna) was photographed on this beautiful line in Arlberg (Austria). It is composed of modern ÖBB carriages that will be connected to Eurocity trains. [5] Included in the Eurocity "Carlo Magno" (Sestri Levante-Dortmund), this German dining car (DB) separates the first-class from the second-class carriages.

[1] The EC train "Bela Bartok," which runs on the Budapest-Frankfurt line, has left Vienna and is heading for Salzburg. It is composed of German and Hungarian coaches.

[2] The CFF in Switzerland obtained a series of 12 first-class panoramic carriages. This one is a part of the EC "Transalpin" (Vienna-Basel) formation.

[Right] The Eurocity train "Ticino" from Zurich is leaving Côme for Milan. Two Swiss panoramic carriages are coupled after the locomotive.

[1] In a homogenous unit train of DB carriages in ICE colours, the EC train "Paganini" is on its way from Verona to Munich.
[2] The Eurocity train "Michelangelo" on the Munich-Rome route. It is made up of a unit train with Italian carriages painted in the colours of FS/Trenitalia.

[3] A stop at a train station in Brig (Switzerland) made by the EC "Monteverdi" on the Geneva-Milan route. The Swiss machine will stay at the head of the train to Domodossola.
[4] The Eurocity "Agram," of recent design, is composed of a unit train with Slovenian, Croatian and Austrian coaches. The picture shows the Croatian dining coach of the HZ company.

[1] The Eurocity train "Catalan-Talgo" (Barcelona-Geneva), previously a TEE, is composed of Spanish "Talgo" carriages whose axles can adapt to various gauges.
[2] Heading from Vienna to Paris, the EC "Mozart" was composed of ÖBB carriages. Today its journeys are limited to Vienna-Munich.

[3] An electric CFF railcar in the grey Eurocity colours is making the TGV Paris-Lausanne connection between Frasne and Berne, the Swiss capital.
[4] The EC "Iris" on its way from Coire to Brussels, arriving at the Strasbourg train station. A Belgian ex-SNCF carriage provides catering on the train.

T he rapid development of interna-tional connections between 1880 and 1900 led to a search for solu-tions adapted to this type of long-distance transport. It is not surprising to observe that the first night trains began running between large cities in the USA.

George Mortimer Pullman showed the way forward in this area. Although they were basic, his carriages provided a high level of comfort. The Belgian Georges Nagelmackers became enthusiastic about this idea and decided to implement it in Europe as well. In 1872, he founded the International Sleeping Carriages Company and put night trains with genuine sleeping coaches into circulation on the main lines of Europe. The opera-tion of the "Orient-Express" train in 1883 marked the beginning of an era of development of this train type. The luxury, perfect service, and very high quality catering guaranteed its success with wealthy clients. Thus, dozens of night trains were put into operation and served the main European capitals. In the 1960s the night trains were democratized. The sleeping cars became less luxurious and the couchette coaches returned in force. Threatened by high-speed trains, various night trains were put out of operation due to a lack of clients. The opera-tors modernized their used equipment. The train-hotels with their air-conditioned carriages and full catering service created a night train renaissance while new entities such as CityNightLine, Artésia and Elipsos were brought into being to exploit those night connections that attracted clientele.

A Night on a Train

The use of private night trains is increasing as the investment required for acquisition of equipment slows down the national compa-nies' programs.

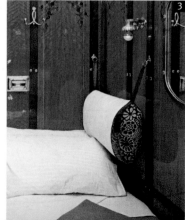

[1] The renovated interior of a sleeping carriage of the AB 30 ex P type operating under the Austrian Railways ÖBB. Similar coaches ran in Belgium and in the Netherlands as well.
[2] A SNCF sleeping carriage of the U type.
[3] The soft and luxurious interior of a CIWL sleeping carriage of the LX type.

[4] A view of a compartment of a Spanish "Talgo" sleeping carriage in a night position. The carriage is rather spartan.
[5] The compartment of a Moroccan couchette coach set in the night-time position.

[1] This notice gives information about a night train line of the "Simplon Orient-Express" running under the name "Taurus Express" to Anatolia.
[2] At the departure from Paris-North, this Danish couchette coach provides a connection to Copenhagen.
[3] This is the night train Stockholm-Narvik, whose running was taken over by a private Swedish company.

[3] A night train coming from Skopje former Yugoslavia is approaching its end station in Munich. It includes couchette coaches and blue sleeping carriages.
[4] The "Wiener Walzer" train is connecting Zurich-Budapest and is composed of sleeping carriages and couchette coaches.

[1] In China, sleeping carriages come in "hard" and "soft" classes. Is any further explanation needed?

[2] The long-distance night train Hoek van Holland (Netherlands)-Klagenfurt (Austria) carried sleeping carriages and couchette coaches.
It was intended primarily for vacationers.

[Right] The night train of the Amtrak company "Coast Starlight" makes the route Seattle-Los Angeles in two days. It is composed of double-decker coaches offering lounges.

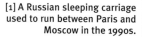

[1] A Russian sleeping carriage used to run between Paris and Moscow in the 1990s.

2] The CFF in Switzerland has couchette coaches available; their exteriors are decorated with stars and a moon.

[3] The night train "Flanders-Riviera" is waiting on a platform at the Brussels-Midi train station before starting the Brussels-Nice journey.

Voiture-lits Carrozza-letti Schlafwagen Sleeping-car

[4] The arrival of a night train, "Stendhal," coming from Paris-Gare-de-Lyon at the Milan-Central station. The sleeping carriages are included at the end of the train.
[5] Taking over the tradition of the Wagon-Lits company, the category of sleeping carriages is indicated in four languages.
[6] Coming from Berlin and Hamburg, this night train of the German DB Nachtzug company arrived at Paris North.

[1] A view into the interior of a compartment of an American sleeping carriage of the "Viewliner" type owned by the Amtrak company.

[2] Coming from Berlin, at that time the capital of East Germany, this sleeping carriage of Mitropa arrived in Vienna, the Austrian capital, the journey's end station.

[3] The night train-hotels of the company CityNightLine offer sleeping carriages on two levels where the upper level is composed of spacious compartments with a corner lounge.

[4] The weekly Bucharest-Paris-East connection made by the famous "Orient-Express" night train was not preserved through lack of sufficient publicity. The picture shows a CFR sleeping carriage at Paris East.

[5] Operated by the French-Italian company Artésia, the night train "Stendhal" coming from Milan arrived at the Paris-Bercy station.

[6] In Japan, where high speed trains reduced the demand for classic trains, night trains experienced a revival with the "Sunrise Express" trains composed of double-decker coaches.

[1] The "Excelsior" sleeping carriage. This type of carriage offers the maximum comfort in its field, providing luxury compartments equipped with an individual shower and a "honeymoon suite."
[2] A SNCF winter-sports train is composed of Corail couchette coaches.
[3] Coming from Brussels, the Belgian couchette coach is approaching Brig, the end station of the journey, included in a domestic train.

[4] Two UH type sleeping carriages with different features are be included in the composition of the "Arlberg Express" night train connecting Paris and Innsbruck (Austria).

[5] The German DB Nachtzug company has unit trains composed of Talgo carriages of Spanish design at its disposal, which work the domestic connections to and from Berlin.

[6] The "Donau Kurier" night train in Dortmund (Germany), going to Vienna. It is operated by the CityNightLine company.

O riginally, due to the short distances between cities served by rail, all trains were regional or local.

Calling at all train stations, they were named "omnibuses" by analogy with stagecoaches serving roadside stations in towns and villages.

Due to the extension of railway services and the birth of express trains, omnibus trains were sidetracked. They were unpopular with operators for a long time because they require large numbers of carriages for a reduced period of utilisation, and in addition they generated low revenue due to tickets being sold at a reduced "social" rate. The operators downgraded equipment on the main lines and invested little. This approach intensified in the 1960s and resulted in a loss of interest in trains. In reality, the clientele became weary of the slowness and basic level of comfort generally offered. Commuters left the rail for the road.

In Europe, it was not until the end of the 1970s that the omnibus trains, which, in the meantime, had become "regional," experienced their revival. This was indicated by the acquisition of new equipment, implementation of more attractive schedules and modernization of train stations. Due to increasing demand, the companies ordered various types of motor railcars, electric railcars and carriages. As they awaited their equipment deliveries, the companies renewed old carriages at high cost in order to offer optimal conditions of comfort. The phenomenon is global. The development of large cities and their suburban services as

Regional Trains

well as interurban short distance connections guarantee the expansion of regional trains operation.

[1] A local train composed of old carriages in the Göteborg network (Sweden).
[2] In the 1960s, this local train seen near Témuco in Chile was pulled by a venerable steam engine.
[3] In the 1960s, an SNCF "omnibus" train is composed of old carriages, some of which are "spoils of war."

[4] An electric railcar of a suburban service in Buenos Aires, the capital of Argentina, also operated by the company FC Mitre.
[5] A picture of a railway station in days of yore in Fleurier (Switzerland), with a railcar of the regional Val de Travers railway.

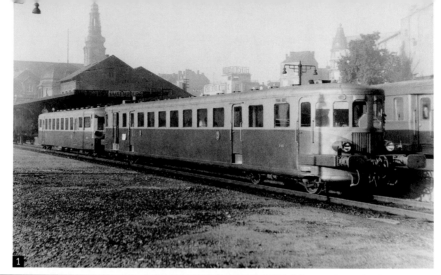

[1] At a train station in Luxembourg in the 1960s, with a French construction railcar.
[2] An electric suburban railcar at the Simon's Town station in Cape Town province, South Africa.

[3] A regional standard gauge train of the Swiss Südostbahn company. It is one of the most active trains in the country.

[4] The suburban trains of Toronto, Canada, are operated by the GO Transit company, utilising mainly double-decker carriages.

[1] A two-axle carriage, used by the ÖBB in Austria for regional services. A large number of those carriages were acquired by tourist railways.

[2] A SNCF carriage called "Bruhat" designed for express services. The series terminated its working career on the omnibus trains.

[3] A CFF regional train has just left Lucerne (Switzerland). The locomotive is pulling the unit train. The driver carriage is at the front.

[Right] Designed for express interurban connections, these stainless steel motor railcars of the Portuguese national company CP were subsequently downgraded to regional connections.

[1] The FS in Italy have received deliveries of railcars of the Aln 668 series since the mid-1960s.
[2] A regional commuter train from Salzburg's local railway. It also transports hikers and holidaymakers.
[3] An electric railcar owned by the WKD provides its services in the outskirts of Warsaw. The company, an old branch of the national PKP, was privatized.

[4] A ÖBB (Austria) railcar of the VT 5047 series, seen near Reutte in the Tyrol, is transporting school children.
[5] A double railcar belonging to DB Regio is waiting for its departure time at the Neustadt train station in the Black Forest (Germany).

[1] Many regional services in Great Britain have been taken over by electric railcars of recent manufacture. They have been distributed among various private operators.

[2] A SNCF double motor railcar unit in the first TER colours at the Givet train station. This vehicle has been renovated and modernized.
[3] The suburban services of Taipei, the capital of Taiwan, were covered by electric railcar train units made in Germany belonging to the national company TRA.

[4] The DB Regio company in charge of regional trains in Germany received new electric railcars, including the two-element ET 426 series.

[5] This electric railcar of the Swiss private company BLS-Lötschbergbahn, intended for regional services, was decorated in the company's livery after its renovation.

[1] A regional train coming from Brig entering the Lausanne station. It is pulled by a CFF electric "NPZ" railcar.

[2] A DB Regio regional train running between Basel and Freiburg (Germany) pulled by a BB of the 146 series. It is of recent manufacture and pulls modernized carriages.

[3] A regional train operating between Milan and Turin with a driver carriage at the front. The machine is pushing the train.

[4] A local train near Zadar, formerly Yugoslavia, and today in Croatia. The American-made diesel locomotive is pulling two axle carriages.

[5] The SNCF received deliveries of the new X 72500 series of motor railcars in a unified TER finish from 1999. One of them may be seen at the Châteaudun train station.

"**U**se the railway for your goods!" was the Swiss Federal Railways' slogan for a very long time, and it reminds us that merchandise has been transported by train since the beginning of the railway era.

Although the railways have greatly contributed to the development of business travel as well as private travel both within and between countries, they also have helped large companies in their development, facilitating the export of their products and the import of raw materials.

Almost anything may be transported by train: wood, coal, ore, fuel oils, cars, iron and steel products, cereals, fruits and vegetables, fish and even radioactive waste!

The rolling stocks of the railways have been diversified due to the variety of products to be transported, thus enhancing their importance. They have been adapted according to specific needs, in particular for the transport of loaded pallets.

Container wagons are experiencing a period of great expansion thanks to their flexibility in utilisation and railway-to-road cooperation. In this area as well, "mobile motorways" – lorries transported by trains, introduced in 1975 – represent a great advance.

Despite a significant reduction in the use of isolated carriages, containers and railway-road techniques are experiencing a peak of utilization. This situation is partially a result

Freight Trains

of liberalism in the field of transportation, which has enabled the establishment of competing private operators.

In Europe, high-speed trains adapted for freight transport represent the next level of development. Fast goods delivery is still awaiting the full development of high-speed networks.

[1] A train fully loaded with coal on the Arlberg line in Austria.
[2] A metric gauge freight train on the Rhaetian Railway, Switzerland.

[3] In the USA the length and weight of the freight trains requires the use of several locomotives, such as here, where four units of the Burlington Northern Santa Fe company are shown.
[4] In South Africa, steam traction no longer serves at the head of freight trains.

[1] A train fully loaded with cereals is pulled by a BBB of the E633 series of FS (Italy).

[2] In Indonesia, this freight train is also used for passenger transport. However, the passengers' security is not guaranteed!

[3] Loading refrigerator wagons on board a ferry crossing Lake Van, Turkey.

[4] A train fully loaded with tanks full of hydrocarbons is pulled by two British diesel locomotives.
[5] A train full of containers is pulled by locomotives belonging to the CP Rail company in Canada, near Toronto.

[1] On certain mountain lines, it is necessary to push locomotives when the total weight of the train is great, as here in Arlberg, Austria.
[2] This heavy train full of coal is operating for a Czech private company. Its traction is provided by two diesel locomotives.

[3] The "Cargo Sprinter" service, composed of motor-driven carriages and transporting containers, never went past the experimental stage. However, it seemed very promising.
[4] The liberalization of railway transport opened the way for CFF Cargo in Switzerland to operate freight trains in Germany. An Re 482 is approaching Freiburg im Breisgau.
[5] A freight train of the NZR company in Zimbabwe, photographed near the famous Victoria Falls.

[1] In the "mobile motorway" system, lorries are transported on special wagons, as here on the line in Tauern, Austria, a region where this highly-developed service has reached its full expansion.

[2] A train belonging to the SNCF cargo company with covered carriages approaches Tours (France). It is capable of reaching speeds of 200 km/h (124 mph).

[3] Seco-Rail, a French private operator in Dourges (France) is moving containers between rail and river transport.

[Right] Certain lines are served only by freight trains, as here in Carpentras (France).

[1] This container, which arrived by lorry, will be loaded onto a wagon by a crane at the Basel-Wolf train station in Switzerland.

[2] From the very first days of the railways, the transport of wood represented a vital element in railway freight traffic. Here in Brig (Switzerland), an important rail junction, wood is being prepared for transport to Italy.

[3] To satisfy special needs, railway companies have been equipped with modern carriages adapted to specific types of transport. The picture shows carriages owned by the Railion DB Logistics company, Germany.

[4] A short freight train is running on a narrow gauge railway for Spoornet, a South African company.
[5] The Arlberg line in Austria is one of the major lines in the European freight network. A train has just arrived at the Landeck station, from where it will start again with a supplementary machine to climb steep slopes.
[6] A train fully loaded with containers, taken by a BB 427 000 of the Fret SNC company, is seen near Avignon.

[1] A freight train is running on the Italy-Austria line of Brenner, another important line in the European network. The wagon with its sliding partitions can carry palleted loads.

[2] A container train with empty containers, pulled by a Belgian B-Cargo machine, is running near Strasbourg and is about to load the containers. It is passing a French Fret SNCF machine.
[3] Fret SNCF, a branch of the French national company, has carriages with mechanical coverings in its service, which are also used for transporting mineral water.

[4] Running on the Italian side of the Brenner line, this train, fully loaded with lorry mobile crates, is going to Verona and Milan.
[5] A considerable volume of goods is also transported on this North-South axis on the Saint-Gothard line between Switzerland and Italy.

Railway
Technology

An interesting system of rails
at the Chaulnes station,
Somme (France).

Rails are fixed on sleepers (or cross-ties), which were originally made of wood. These are embedded in ballast, a layer of stone that spreads the pressure generated by trains running on them and maintains the exact path of the line.

However, apart from rails, sleepers, and ballast, lines have little in common. Very different types of rail gauge were and still are used around the world.

The 1.435 m (4.7 ft.) gauge, known as "standard gauge," is in most widespread use. It was established according to the wheel gauge of stagecoaches of yesteryear, and was chosen by George Stephenson in 1825. Other gauges, corresponding to various criteria, can sometimes be found on the same continent.

These may survive even today, as they provide for exchanges among networks. Military strategy concerns played an important role in the selection of gauges at the time when railway projects were being projected and implemented.

Next in the family of track types are the "narrow gauge lines," of which a meter gauge, also called a "metric gauge," is most widely used. It is commonly used in Western Europe, in particular in Switzerland, but it may also often be seen in Asia and South America.

The other components of this category are the "military" gauge tracks of 0.60 m (1.96 ft.), were most often used by factories in the past; these tracks were established in Austria, Yugoslavia, Romania and Bulgaria.

Railway Lines

Finally, the list of gauges is completed with the 0.75 m (2.46 ft.) and 0.90 m (2.95 ft.) gauge lines often found in Poland. The 0.381 m (1.25 ft.) gauge is generally used on amusement park railways such as the Wiener Prater in the Austrian capital.

[1] The construction of the Trans-Siberian Railway in Russia was carried out between 1891 and 1915.
After its completion, the line connected Moscow and Vladivostok along a route 5,695 miles long!
[2] A standard gauge line at the CFF train station in Montreux, Switzerland.

[3] A Spanish suburban train is running at a broad gauge of 1.676 m (5.49 ft.).
[4] The gauge of the St. Pölten line in Mariazell, Austria, is 0.76 m (2.49 ft.).
[5] A venerable steam engine on the Pithiviers line (France) at a 0.60 m (1.97 ft.) gauge.

[1] The Argentinean railway network runs on a broad gauge of 1.676 m (5.49 ft.).
[2] In China, the majority of the railways run at a 1.524 m (5 ft.) gauge.
[3] The gauge of the Australian network in Queensland is 1.067 m (3.5 ft.).

[4] The line in Zermatt, Switzerland, runs at a metric gauge, and is partially equipped with a rack rail mounted on the sleepers.
[5] This Indonesian steam locomotive runs at a 1.067 m (3.5 ft.) gauge.
[6] The Blanc-Argent line, France, is a metric gauge line.

[1] A Swiss electric railcar at a metric gauge is pulling a standard-gauge carriage placed on a carriage truck.
[2] A steam 0.75 m (2.5 ft.) gauge locomotive on one of the secondary lines in Saxony, Germany.

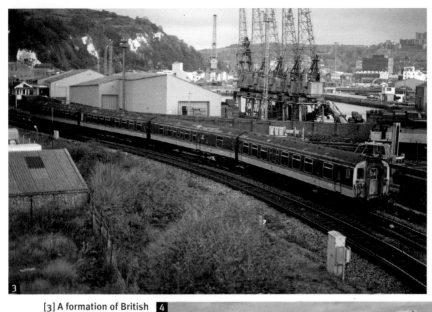

[3] A formation of British electric railcars supplied by a third lateral rail is arriving at Dover.

[4] The Canadian railway network is built at the standard gauge. The illustration shows a passenger train from the Ontario Northland Railway company.

[1] A diesel locomotive on a metric gauge track at the depot in Chernex. The machine is owned by the Swiss company Montreux-Oberland Bernois.

[2] A Finnish steam engine at a 1.524 m (5 ft.) gauge.
[3] This small German shunter is running at a 0.50 m (1.64 ft.) gauge, which was created within the enclosure of a museum in Neuenmarkt-Wirsberg.

[4] Two diesel locomotives of the NZR company in Zimbabwe on a network using the 1.067 m (3.5 ft.) gauge.
[5] The Liliputbahn in Prater park, Vienna, runs at a narrow gauge of 0.381 m (1.25 ft.).

[1] Power supply by a third lateral rail on the line of Saint-Gervais-Vallorcine.

[2] A locomotive that works on maintenance of overhead lines on a standard gauge railway in Germany.
[3] In India, many secondary lines work at a 1.067 m (3.5 ft.) gauge.
[Right] An electric railcar on a suburban tram line in Saint-Florian is running at a 0.90 m (2.95 ft.) gauge.

[1] The metric gauge of the Rhaetian Railway and the CFF standard gauge join at Coire station (Switzerland).
[2] A gauge renovation locomotive is traversing the train station in Mans, transported by a freight train.

[3] A diesel locomotive at a 1.524 m (5 ft.) gauge on the Armenian railway network.
[4] A Bulgarian electric locomotive, made in Romania, is pulling a freight train.
[5] Two Israeli Railways diesel motor railcars from a standard gauge network.

An example of old signaling
technology is on display in the
Nuremberg museum
(Germany).

S ince the commissioning of the first railway lines there has been a dilemma in transmitting orders to engine drivers. Should they be informed that the line is free – thus guaranteeing safety first – or given information about speed and direction?

At the dawn of railway transport, the task of signaling was performed by individuals distributed along the lines. They were responsible for watching single points such as level crossings or the distances between trains.

Provided with flags during the day and lamps at night, the signalers were also equipped with whistles for conveying orders. The crudeness of the signals led to the introduction of optical signals operated on the spot and then at a distance. These were chiefly introduced on the main railway lines.

Semaphores, discs and squares of various colours appeared along the lines. At night the signals were lit up with oil lamps, then with petrol lamps, and later with electric lights. In addition, traffic lights were introduced, which were operated from a signal box. This electric stationing technology ensures an appropriate distance between trains.

It was not easy to unify the colour code, but new technologies have already been created with the signaling equipment mounted on board the traction locomotives of high-speed trains, which leads to the phasing out of classic signals along the lines. In the future, thanks to satellites and

Signaling

the ERMTS system, train traffic will be regulated more efficiently. Classic signaling will still remain in use on important lines, but with enhanced safety.

[1] A main signal is securing the exit from the Zermat train station in Switzerland.
[2] A red SNCF light disc near Longueau.

[3] Seen from the driver's cabin of a locomotive, this light signal indicates a clear way (green light).
[4] The main signal at the exit from the train station of Campo di Trens/Frienfeld (Italy).
[5] An old Swiss signal system, with a main signal on two palettes and an advanced signal on a signal arm.

[1] This Egyptian signal gantry is of British origin.
[2] In Argentina, a train is passing on the right of a mechanical signal in a closed position.
[3] The signal gantries at Charing Cross station in London.

[4] The Bavarian-type mechanical semaphores at the Garmisch-Partenkirchen station (Germany).
[5] A section signalling device on a high-speed line in France.
[6] This command post in Charleroi (Belgium) is in charge of signals and rail switches.

[1] Detail of a new main light signal at a station in Garmisch-Partenkirchen in Bavaria. It indicates a "stop".
[2] At the Châteaudun station (France), "square" mechanical signals, speed signs and order execution signs (Z).
[3] A Swiss CFF light signal at the exit from a train station. Right] In the past at the Sarreguemines station (France) where the semaphores from Alsace-Lorraine and SNCF "squares" of SNCF meet.

[1] In Spain, this beautiful signal gantry presents various mechanical signals.
[2] A British signal by a switch and signalling post.

[3] This train station was equipped with mechanical semaphores.
[4] A mechanical signal at a station museum in Hays, Canada.
[5] An interior view from a command post in operation in the OHE network near Hanover (Germany). From this point on, the line is operated by remote control.

[1] At the Luxembourg train station these out-of-order mechanical signals recall the past.
[2] A beautiful example of a "candlestick" in Belgium with a portal frame holding mechanical signs.
[3] An example of a modern signal gantry in Austria, with the main ÖBB signal.

[4] Another example of a signal gantry holding mechanical signals in the Netherlands.
[5] A nice assembly of mechanical signals may be seen in the French Museum of Railways in Mulhouse.
[6] This main signal protects the entry to the train station in Ober Grafendorf on the Mariazell line (Austria).

The Montenvers railway
(France) was operated
by steam locomotives
until the 1950s.

Railway developers often became reckless in their designs for planned connections. Tunnels, bridges, elevated tracks or high embankments accompanied many lines, especially in the mountains. The invention of a cog rail proved to be a great improvement.

This type of line was seen for the first time in Switzerland as a result of the initiative of Niklaus Riggenbach. In 1871, he put the first cog line into operation to climb the slopes of Mont Rigi. Riggenbach's invention consisted of two parallel rails, in the middle of which bars with a trapezoidal cross-section constituted a kind of ladder that meshed with the toothed driving cogwheel. Other systems made by Abt and Strüb were also developed.

As an adaptable mountain-rail solution adapted for the occasion, the cog railway was quickly developed in Europe, especially in France, Austria, and Germany, but most of all in Switzerland. Moreover, the steepest rail track in the world is found in Swiss territory, climbing Mont Pilat.

Although steam traction was chosen for a good number of lines, electric rail was developed and improved the performance. Nonetheless, steam traction did not disappear from these lines, as the nostalgic atmosphere attracts many tourists who visit from all over the world.

Despite principally providing for passenger traffic, certain cog railway lines also handle freight traffic, transporting foodstuffs and other necessary products in the direction

Cog Railways

of mountain peaks where hotels and restaurants are often located.

Schynige Platte. — Bahn. Eiger, Mönch und Jungfrau.

[1] Near Bucova in Romania, this steam train on a standard gauge line enters onto part of a cog rail signaled by a lamp on the right.
[2] The locomotive No. 3 of Achenseebahn at the Jenbach train station (Austria).
[3] A steam train of the Swiss company named Schynige Platte Bahn amidst magnificent surroundings.

[4] In the USA, the "Manitou-Pike's Peak Railway" uses diesel railcars manufactured in Switzerland.
[5] An electric train of the Swiss company Montreux-Glion, a line that has been electrified since its beginning.
[6] An electric railcar at a metric gauge owned by the German company Wendelsteinbahn, manufactured in Switzerland.

[1] A train of the company Berner-Oberland Bahnen, which uses a metric gauge, is arriving at the Lauterbrunnen station (Switzerland).

[2] The metric gauge cog railway trains belonging to the Bayerische Zugspitzbahn company, Bavaria, carry tourists to the highest mountain in Germany.
[3] A steam train belonging to the Swiss company Brienz-Rothorn Bahn, at a 0.80 m (2.6 ft.) gauge.
[Right] An electric railcar of the Martigny-Châtelard company on a cog rail section.

[1] A cog rail switch on the railway of Rhone (France).

[2] To climb Zermatt, the metric gauge line owned by BVZ (Switzerland) uses various cog rail parts.
[3] Mount Rigi in Switzerland is accessible by two standard gauge lines equipped with a cog rail.

[4] The Schneeberg railway (Austria) put interesting metric gauge motor railcars into operation. They are called Salamanders because of their finish.

[5] This picturesque equipment is still in operation on the Rhune railway in Pyrenees.

[6] Switzerland is a mountainous countryand therefore has numerous cog rail systems. The Wengernalpbahn railway is equipped with cog rails.

[1] This steam cog engine at a 0.75 m (2.46 ft.) gauge is on display near Athens.
[2] The Mont Pilat railway in Switzerlan offers the highest downslope gradient in the world, at 48%!
[3] One of the last steam operations on the Montenvers line near Chamonix.

[4] The famous "Glacier Express" is able to cross over the Furka mountain pass in Switzerland due to its cog rail.
[5] A metric gauge railway leads to Monte Generoso, Switzerland.

The idea of public city transport is not a new one. Pascal invented a system for Paris, and started to test it in 1665. However, the idea was not brought to life until the 19th century.

In 1825, carriages pulled by horses worked in Nantes. Subsequently, this technique was developed in Brussels, Berlin and Paris, where six thousand horses were needed! However, the horse-drawn vehicles faced poor quality carriageways, which hinded their efficient operation. In 1853, the first genuine tramway appeared as the "American railway" in New York. It quickly overthrew horse-drawn traction as it was more flexible in use – although the aerial supply in the city-center caused certain problems. It was only accepted at the end of the 19th century. In the meanwhile, the networks were expanded and the widest network, with 753 km of lines and more than two thousand electric railcars, was to be found in Philadelphia in 1889.

Electric traction revolutionized urban transportation. Many networks now branch out beyond city limits and reach into the suburbs. As with other railway types, different rail gauges and systems are used.

The development of automobiles after the Second World War resulted in the decline of the tramways, except in those towns where tramway transport operated separately from the automobile routes.

Deluged in road traffic, large cities are resorting to tramways again. They operate on adjusted lines and are no longer bedevilled by traffic jams. The frequency and

From Horse to Tramway

rapidity of the tramways' operation increases, thus leading to a renewal of this type of transport, once written off as "obsolete."

2 [1] An old tram in Basel is providing a historic service. [2] This horse-driven tram is on display in the Transport Museum in Brussels.

[3] An old construction tram in Rome, where this equipment was in operation for an exceptionally long period of time.

[4] Thanks to the French Amitram association, this horse-driven tram recalls the early days of public transport.

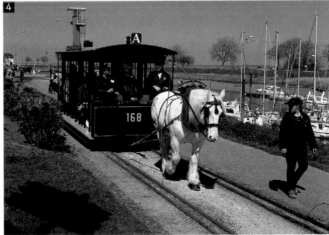

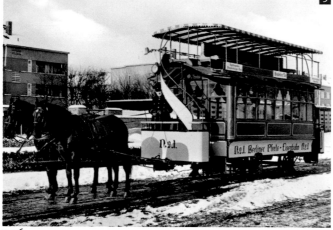

[1] This old tram in Vienna serves as a sign for a McDonald's restaurant in Reutte (Austria). [2] Dating back to the 1950s, this tram used to run in Toronto. [3] In Berlin, too, horse-driven trams provided public transport.

[4] One of the first electric trams in Berlin. It was preserved as a historic locomotive.
[5] In Portugal, Porto owns a charming tram network.
[6] A tram from the 1960s in Nagasaki, Japan.

[1] A two-element train unit and trailer from the 1950s are operating in the streets of Nuremberg (Germany).

[2] Operating on their "own place" means on a line reserved only for trams. This tram unit in Brussels does not encounter any operational problems.
[3] There is a vast network of trams in Vienna.
[Right] Motor railcars put out of operation were transported to Paraguay and renewed their operation in the Asunción network.

3 [1] "Mongy," the Lille-Roubaix-Tourcoing line, has been modernized and performs a complementary function in the public transport organization.
[2] One of the shortest tram lines in Europe is found in Gmunden (Austria). It is being extended.
[3] In Valencia (Spain), the tram network was given large capacity modern vehicles.

[4] The "cable-car" of San Francisco, opened in 1873, is a mobile historical monument. Driven by a cable, it runs up and down streets along breathtaking slopes.

[5] The return of trams in France also took place in Rouen, where the network is integrated into the "Metrobus" system.

[6] In Amsterdam, the line 20, called the "Circle Tram," makes the rounds of the main monuments of the city and serves visiting tourists.

[1] Countries where individual motorisation is not (yet) very developed, enhance their public transport networks as here in Sofia, Bulgaria.
[2] Grenoble, the Dauphine capital, has adopted the tram as a solution to traffic problems.
[3] The town of Bordeaux opted for the tram as well.

[4] Already possessing a vast network of underground lines, Moscow also developed its tram network, in particular on branches reaching out to the suburbs.
[5] An interesting snowplow tram was photographed in Harbin, China.

353

The continuous urbanization of large cities at the end of the 19th century caused many problems for responsible politicians and economists. The necessity of inventing other systems of transport soon became evident.

The first steam traction metro line – the Tube – was born in London in 1862.

Other cities also began their own to construct lines and networks. The first line in continental Europe was opened in Budapest in 1896; in Paris, another line was opened between Vincennes and the Maillot Gate in July 1900. A private company also opened a new underground service between Saint-Lazare and Porte-de-Versailles; it was called the Nord-Sud. The construction of various networks was completed in 1914 except for the luxurious Moscow metro, which experienced delays and opened in the 1930s.

The decline of the tramways may be explained in the majority of cases by automobile transit development after the Second World War. In Brussels and other large cities, the same tramways continued to operate, becoming either a "pre-metro" or a "light rail" system.

However, because of the constantly increasing car flow, large cities are obliged to return to more effective public transport. The use of tramways has been renewed but the construction of new metro lines runs up against a determining factor: the price.

In various European cities, the transport system plan includes the development of tramways as well as underground lines,

Underground Transport

such as in Vienna, Austria, and various German cities. Automatic light rail systems have also appeared. Now, research on the optimal quality of life in various large cities casts doubts on the widespread use of cars. Urban public transport will experience a period of expansion once again.

[1] Modern architecture for the Singapore Metro.

[2] The construction of the Metro in Paris began in 1900 and was later expanded. The picture shows the site near the Opera station where several lines will cross.

[3] In Vienna, various metro lines complete the public transport network of the Austrian capital.

[4] This old Paris Metro railcar was restored to its original condition and appearance.
[5] There are also metro lines in Rome.

357

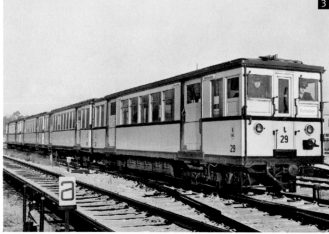

[1] In Athens, two generations of metro equipment in a chance meeting.
[2] An interesting electric metro railcar in Budapest.
[3] Berlin opted for a city metro network in the 1930s.

[4] Toronto, the capital city of Ontario in Canada, has, in addition to tramway lines, a municipal underground network.
[5] In Marseille (France), the metro employs a technology with train units running on pneumatic tyres.

[1] The French capital has a vast Metro network at its command. Vehicles run on both pneumatic tires and classical wheels.

[2] The city of Brussels is also equipped with metro lines.
[3] In Lille, an automatic metro network of the VAL type is used. It also employs the technology of pneumatic tires on rails.
[Right] The reunification of Germany and Berlin included a reorganisation of the city metro network.

[1] In Paris, the extension of Metro lines has made it possible to travel beyond the capital city's limits, for example to the Défense.

[2] An example of a German underground line in Essen an der Ruhr.

[3] Although the metro lines described above are all urban, certain cities also operate suburban lines, such as New York.

[4] The London underground's nickname, the "Tube," comes from its narrow measurement.
[5] In Charleroi, the modernization of tramway lines was accompanied by the "pre-metro" appellation. Train units running on classical tramways work there, but using improved infrastructure.
[6] Certain lines of the Paris Metro run above the ground as an "aerial metro."

363

[1] The success of underground transport in Vienna enabled the construction of new lines complementing those lines developed in the past as the "Stadtbahn" or urban railway.

[2] The high price of constructing metro lines has slowed down many intended extensions, such as in Athens where the suburban tramway then gained favor.

[3] Despite having
a well-developed tramway
network, Amsterdam also
invested in a classic metro.
[4] Of French design, this system
running on pneumatic tires
evolved in Santiago,
the capital of Chile.

Paris commands the vast train
network of the Regional
Express Network (RER).

The first organised suburban rail system was introduced in Berlin in 1924. The expansion of cities has led to research in the field of urban mass transport systems. Various solutions are proposed to respond to this demand.

The ongoing development of various large cities leads to finding ways to make a reduction in the number of cars on the city streets possible.

Since the 1970s, many networks of express regional trains have been introduced into public transport with the Parisian RER by SNCF and RATP. They are introduced into many German cities (Munich, Frankfurt, and Cologne) and in Austria (Vienna) and then in Switzerland (Zurich and Berne). Having been made accessible to the masses thanks to favourable tariff conditions, the S-Bahn and RER lines experience increasing passenger rates.

Although suburban lines are also being revitalized or built new in the USA and Japan, the tram-train technology appearing in Europe at the beginning of the 1990s is a small revolution in the sector.

Capable of running in city centers and also in the suburban agglomerations, the train units of a "tram-train" avoid the problem of slack time, as they largely facilitate a home-to-work (and vice versa) commuting pattern. This futuristic technology appeared in Karlsruhe, Germany, and was imitated in Saarbrucken and also in France.

Innovation in the world of railway transport has not ended; it is reasonable to expect that many solutions now still in the planning stages will, some day, be integral to the

Suburban Trains

solutions of how to best facilitate regular movements of the population.

[1] Known in the past as the "Sceaux line," this line was integrated in the RER network after the modernization of infrastructures and equipment.
[2] The local railway from Cologne to Bonn (Germany) was working on its own line. It has since been integrated in the tramway network.
[3] Stockholm also boasts a network of suburban lines.

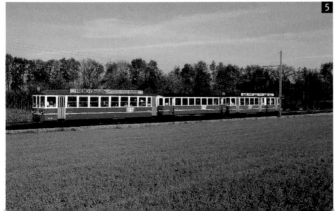

[4] In Boston, the Green Line is an underground line employing train units of tram-type light carriages.

[5] The tramway line 17 in Basel is a suburban line of Basel, and a line in Alsace at the same time.

369

[1] The Viennese "Stadtbahn" network was integrated into the underground after its modernisation and complete reconstruction.

[2] The RER train units operated by the RATP originally had a unique look. Since then, they have found it beneficial to give their trains the same look as two other operators.

[3] The vast S-Bahn lines network of Berlin were restored after the reunification of Germany and new equipment was put into operation.

[4] The S-Bahn network in Berlin is also used for commuting from home to work and back, and more spacious and comfortable train units replaced the old equipment.

[5] The Munich network also connects holiday resorts such as here at the Starnberg lake, to the south of the Bavarian capital.

[1] The evolution, or even revolution, of the operation of trams on suburban lines of DB in Germany.

[2] In Germany, the Freibourg-Elzach suburban line also handles sightseeing transport on the Breisgau-S-Bahn with train units called Regioshuttle.
[3] The S-Bahn in Zurich uses the CFF double-decker equipment.
[Right] A suburban train headed for Oslo's outskirts is just about to leave.

[1] In Cairo, "Métro" train units of French origin run on suburban lines.

[2] The Dutch town of Utrecht acquired a fast suburban tramway line that joins the periphery with the town centre.

[3] Lausanne built up the East-West line in order to relieve the traffic congestion in the center and to serve the surrounding areas.

[4] Using modern equipment, the S-Bahn network in Vienna successfully developed alongside its population.
[5] A vast network of suburban lines is used in Sydney, Australia.

[1] The RER and suburban Parisian network is integrated in the "Transilien" group.
[2] SNCF ordered many electric double-decker railcar train units to meet the demand for service on the RER network in Paris.
[3] As an important economic metropolis, the city of Hamburg is served by an S-Bahn type train network.

[4] In San Diego in the USA, a suburban line network is operated by light electric railcars of a "pre-metro" design.
[5] In Geneva, a suburban line to the Plaine is used under the RER name.

377

Nostalgic
Journeys

T he end of the 1960s heard death knells ring for a large number of secondary lines all across Europe. Considerable investment would have been necessary to save them, but many governments of that time preferentially allocated resources to road transport, to the detriment of railway services.

Countless small rural lines were abandoned due to the lack of investment.

The trains stopped, the train station closed, and then the closure of shops and later even the village school often followed. The rural exodus affected many European countries and whole regions became depopulated. The railway line closures were farewell events organised by associations of train enthusiasts. Despite being comparatively few in number, they created the notion of railway heritage.

Thanks to the activities of the associations, in a slightly more than a quarter of a century, several hundred lines in various European countries such as France, Germany, Belgium, Austria and Great Britain were preserved. The USA is not far behind, and follows the movement. Various lines serving famous tourist regions will be "reactivated" after several years of neglect. The list of achievements is impressive; however, the failures, are also numerous.

Certain lines will survive for only a few summers, their place lost to to cycle paths under local policies. The tourist railways participate in the local economies of their regions, but beyond their recreational character, they remain above all key witnesses to global railway history. Far from being marginal, the phenomenon has spread, proving that nostalgia has always had its supporters.

Rebirth

[1] The Mure railway (France) is one of the most picturesque lines in all of Europe.
[2] One of the oldest tourist railways, the "Ffestiniog Railway", in Great Britain, at a 0.60 m (1.96 ft.) gauge.

[3] In the USA, the Durango-Silverton railway is a very popular attraction. Traction is provided by steam locomotives. [4] The Three-Valley railway in Belgium manages a sizeable fleet of traction vehicles, from which steam locomotives of various origins come to the fore.

[1] A tourist train in Valencia (Spain) pulled by a steam locomotive.
[2] On the tourist railway of the Taurachbahn in Austria, a train pulled by the 298.56 steam locomotive has just arrived at the Mauterndorf station.
[3] An old forest network became a railway in the USA, the "Roaring Camp Big Trees Railway."

384

4

5

[4] To provide for a journey in "retro" style, the tourist railways renovate old cars. This one, running on the Endingen line in Germany, dates back to the beginning of the 20 th century.

[5] This old two-axle carriage and the open platforms are part of the beautiful collection of tourist train association in Endingen (Germany).

385

[1] An amateur mechanic driving a diesel locomotive. The drivers' qualifications are strictly monitored.

[2] In the Netherlands, this steam locomotive is running on the Boekelo line.

[3] The Vennbahn railway (Belgium) commands a vast network where trains equipped with dining coaches run on the main lines.

[Right] In the Basque Country, a line closed to passenger traffic could be renewed in the summer as a tourist railway.

[1] This tourist railway near Grenoble runs on a former industrial line.

[2] The "La Traction" organisation operates steam trains on the railways of Jura in Switzerland.
[3] South Africa has also developed a notion of railway heritage. This photograph of a historic train was taken in Port Elizabeth.

[4] Originating in an industrial network, this steam locomotive took over operation on a tourist line near Essen (Germany).
[5] Old carriages run on a museum line of the Grand Canyon Railway in the USA. Perfectly maintained, they evoke reminiscences of travelling in the past.

[1] A Jagsttalbahn shunter is shunting at Dörzbach train station (Germany), a line also used for tourist traffic.
[2] In Brazil, this steam locomotive pulls historical trains on a narrow gauge track.
[3] The Transport Museum in Brussels organises tourist trips featuring the use of historical equipment.

[4] In Volos, Greece, enthuslasts are starting to renovate a steam locomotive that they will return to operation on a tourist line in Peillon.
[5] A diesel train on the tourist railway of Vermandois in Saint Quentin (France). This locomotive comes from SNCF and was saved from scrap.
[6] On tourist networks safety is crucial; here is a protected crossing on the Froissy-Cappy line in the Somme.

One of the most interesting
railway museums in Europe is
located in York (Great Britain).

T here are many rail museums in the world, especially in Europe, the birthplace of railways. They bear witness to the past by means of railway equipment, pictures and accessories. An impressive heritage has been preserved in the enduring equipment, buildings, artwork...

In York, Great Britain; Mulhouse, France; Lucerne in Switzerland; in Strasshof, near Vienna, Austria, the collections have been evaluated, and often completed with every model maker's dream models. Whether museum exhibits are railway collections such as STET Cité du Train or the Rail Transport Museum of New Delhi, India, model presentations tracing the development of transport from ferry to railcar, as in Järnvägsmuseum in Stockholm, or special galleries devoted to trains, such as the Science Museum in London or the National Museum of Science and Technology in Milan, there are many possibilities for making railway history discoveries. Such museums may also be found in Sacramento, Helsinki (Finland), Brussels (Belgium), Santiago (Chile), Barcelona and Madrid (Spain), Saint Constant (Québec), Utrecht (Netherlands), Berlin, Bochum, Neustadt and Nuremberg (Germany).

Multiple initiatives involving tourist railways may be found on a regional scale, for example, in the museum of narrow gauge

Museums

lines in Froissy-Cappy in the county of Somme, France; in Blumberg, Germany; or in Treignes, Belgian Ardennes. And these projects do not miss their mark. The enthusiast can only be delighted by the choices available.

[2] [1] This ex-SNCF BB 12000 series is a part of an impressive collection presented in the Cité du Train in Mulhouse (France). [2] One of the showrooms in the Nuremberg museum in Germany.

[3] In Strasshof (Austria), a collection of locomotives in working condition is on display in this old depot transformed into a museum.
[4] In Nördlingen (Germany) an old depot became a Bavarian Railway museum.

3

[1] In Villanova (Spain), the historical steam locomotives are on display in the open air in an engine shed.
[2] Now located in Lucerne's Swiss Transport Museum, this locomotive from 1881 used to run on the Saint-Gothard line.
[3] In Utrecht, (the Netherlands), this dining coach in resplendent teak, previously owned by the Sleeping Carriages Company, is a part of a superb collection now on display to the public.

[4] The National Railway Museum has been established in Odensee (Denmark).
[5] The museum belonging to the tourist Blonay-Chamby railway presents various locomotives of Swiss origin.
[6] Part of the history of steam traction in Poland is on display at the Warsaw train station.

[1] In Vienna, is a museum devoted to public transport features in particular many old trams.
[2] In Delhi, India, railway history is presented in the open air in the form of historical locomotives.
[Right] In Australia, various historical locomotives and equipment are shown in the open air in Melbourne.

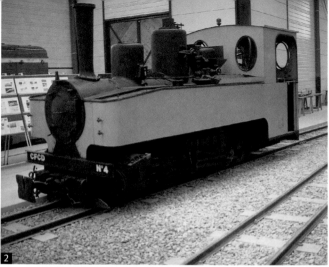

[1] In a railway museum in Treignes, Belgium, equipment of various provenances is on display, such as this locomotive from Luxembourg.
[2] In Froissy (France), an interesting museum traces the history of the 0.60 m (1.97 ft.) gauge line.
[3] One of the most interesting equipment collections may be seen in the Cité du Train in Mulhouse (France).

[4] This elegant steam locomotive is a part of the collection to be seen in a museum in Delhi.
[5] The Mining Centre in Lewarde (France) displays various locomotives previously used in the mines.
[6] In Sacramento, California, various locomotives are also on display in the open air.

[1] In Villanova (Spain), some locomotives are also shown under a shelter.
[2] This historical shunter is owned by the Denis-Papin Centre in Oignies (France).
[3] This impressive 241 type locomotive is on display in Santiago, Chile.

[4] An old CFF dining coach serves as a restaurant on the premises of the Swiss Transport Museum in Lucerne.
[5] A small narrow gauge steam engine is also presented in Santiago, Chile.
[6] The well-lit exhibition halls of the Swiss Transport Museum in Lucerne show historical locomotives with accuracy.

Cows watch a train passing
through, in Poland on a
special journey.

The notion of railway heritage has inspired the circulation of special chartered trains by amateurs and enthusiasts. Put into operation on special occasions such as line or train anniversaries, they invigorate the main lines as secondary axes.

Although the enthusiasts regularly ride on special trains of all types (though mostly those drawn by steam traction), cinema and television also participate in this type of service. In reality, old trains, no matter how they look, allow for recreating the atmosphere of the 1950s, or even earlier.

An extensive collection of locomotives, coaches, and wagons enables variety in the choice of equipment.

Tourist railways are also often chosen for this type of footage.

Many organisations depend on national companies to put various special historical trains into operation. These include the SBB-Historic and Classic Rail in Switzerland, the DB Museum in Germany, and the ÖBB/Erlebnisbahn in Austria. In France, it is the associations that operate in this field, although it is possible that an organisation may also be created by SNCF. On the American continent, various societies have appeared with the aim of maintaining the historical equipment intended for this type of service.

Although special trains were limited to a few journeys at first, they gained popularity and were put into operation on weekends, and

Special Trains

later also during the week. This frequency opened the way for the creation of charter companies whose development is the answer to rapidly-increasing demand.

[1] An old SNCF railcar of the VH type departing from Dijon is making a special journey for enthusiasts.
[2] The steam locomotive 38.1772 is pulling a special amateur train near Lengerich, Germany.

[3] Bourgogne and Franche-Comté, a French association, put their historical railcars into operation for the benefit of enthusiasts and works councils.

[4] In this Romanian forest network, a track motorcar serves to transport tourists on request.

[5] Coming from Paris, this AJECTA special train has entered Belgium and is going to Mariembourg.

[1] A detail of a preserved steam locomotive of the 475 series belonging to Czech Railways.
[2] In Argentina, the demand for special trains has made it possible to restore historic locomotives like this impressive machine of the 241 type to their original condition.
[3] The 1020 series historic locomotive owned by ÖBB-Nostalgia is pulling a special train to Innsbruck (Austria).

[4] A beautifully renovated special chartered train pulled by the X 4449 "Daylight." It is composed of historic carriages made by the Southern Pacific company (USA).
[5] After years of motionlessness, the 140 C 27 belonging to CITEV, France, is making a test run after being restored to operational condition.

[1] In Northern Ireland, a steam traction train for enthusiasts returns to Belfast.

[2] The Bavarian Railway Museum in Nördlingen put several historic trains into operation, including some with electric drive.

[Right] Composed of historical carriages formerly belonging to the Sleeping Carriages Company, this special train is pulled by a steam locomotive owned by the Spanish association AZAFT.

3

[1] Double traction by steam locomotives for an enthusiasts' train in the Czech Republic.

[2] A historic steam locomotive is leading a special train in Jonköping (Sweden).

[3] Special trains for enthusiasts run on various narrow-gauge lines in Poland on specific dates or by request.

[4] A regular steam train, owned by the Harzbahnen company (Germany), is running next to a special chartered train. The trains are photographed where the two lines divide.

[5] The ÖBB Nostalgia department operates various historic locomotives on fixed dates, such as this railcar photographed on the Semmering line.

[6] The operation of special trains for international service was not easy in the past. This steam traction train is heading for San Remo (Italy) after having left Nice.

413

[1] The 230 G 353 was the last SNCF steam locomotive preserved for historic trains or the cinema.
[2] A train unit made of 1st class coaches and one Pullman carriage is coupled onto a SNCF CC 65500 during a circular tour around Paris.

[3] Thanks to a local association, the RhB's renovated historic equipment is running on a steep and beautiful Bernina line, Grisons (Switzerland).
[4] In Spain, this impressive 141 F type steam locomotive is pulling a special train.

While the railway was in full decline, the notion of "nostalgia" appeared. It resulted in a demand for different, comfortable, or even luxurious trains. Therefore, luxury trains reappeared after decades of absence.

The operation of a comfort train between Zurich and Istanbul in 1976 was the first sign of the luxury trains' comeback. In 1977 the Swiss Albert Glatt decides to put comfortable and luxurious trains back into operation. His "Nostalgia Istanbul Orient Express" enjoys considerable commercial success, and heralded the arrival of other trains of the same type.

Five years later, the "Venice-Simplon Orient Express" started its operation, soon followed by its Iberian version "Al Andalus Expreso." All these trains are composed of historic carriages renovated at great expense and offering incomparable comfort. The famous Sleeping Carriages Company followed the movement and came out with the "Pullman Orient Express."

The phenomenon of luxury trains crossed the European borders and reached South Africa with the "Blue Train" or "Rovos Rail" and also the USA where "dinner trains" are very popular. In Asia, the "Eastern and Oriental Express" is distinguished by its service and "dream journey."

The clientele for this type of train proved to be of utmost importance; this is why the initiatives succed. So the validity of the initial idea of George Nackelmacker – the

From Comfort to Luxury

CIWL creator – is verified, whose ambition was to offer the travelling on the best conditions with regard to the comfort, services and catering.

The luxury trains of today maintain this lifestyle in the most agreeable of ways. There is a certain price, but the dream is often priceless.

[1] The luxury train "Andalus Expreso" at Granada (Spain).

[2] Chic and delightful service on board the "Wild Life Express" train in Sweden.
[3] A view of a cabin on board the British luxury train, the "Royal Scotsman."

418

[4] Cruising in a postcard landscape – Arlberg, Austria – the luxury train Venice-Simplon Orient Express is running to Saint-Anton and Paris.

[5] Serving petit-fours in a cosy atmosphere of muffled voices on board a unit train chartered by SNCF in France.

[6] The "Great South Pacific" luxury train offered maximum comfort.

[1] Detail of the dining coach of a luxury train, the "Palace on Wheels" in India.

[2] Operated by a charter company based in France, the carriage "Le Salon Bleu" offers elegant comfort.

[3] A panoramic view on board of an air-conditioned carriage of the "Crystal Panoramic Express" running between Montreux and Zweisimmen in Switzerland.

[Right] Renamed the "Golden Pass Express," the panoramic carriage train of the Berne Montreux-Oberland company allows another approach to the countryside.

[1] Detail of a Pullman carriage of the English unit train from the "Venice Simplon Orient Express."

[2] The panoramic carriage service allows discoveries along the Bernina line of the Rhaetian Railway, Switzerland, one of the most scenic countries in Europe.

[3] The "Blue Train" is a luxury train in South Africa.

[4] The "Pullman" inscription on this carriage guaranteed comfort with exquisite attention to detail on board the "Pullman Orient Express" train.
[5] Shown in the preceding picture: view of the interior of one of the Pullman carriages of a French luxury train.
[6] The luxury trains offer maximum comfort, pampering services and very sophisticated cuisine. This is the dining carriage of the "Blue Train," South Africa.

[1] The famous "Glacier Express" connects Zermatt and Saint-Moritz in Switzerland. A high-class dining carriage folllows the locomotive.

[2] On the board a Spanish train, the "Andalus Expreso," the comfort contributes to a change of scene.
[3] Traversing through enchanting country, the "Royal Scotsman" train takes in only a small number of passengers to ensure optimal comfort.

[4] The breakfast service on board the Spanish luxury train "Transcantabrico" running at a metric gauge. The train also includes sleeping cars.
[5] The piano bar atmosphere on board the carriage Pullman of the ÖBB-Nostalgia company.
[6] These American panoramic carriages allows one to enjoy a different kind of journey.

[1] On board the train "Golden Pass Classic," the duration of journey between Montreux and Zweisimmen seems to be shorter.
[2] The luxury "British Pullman" train runs on fixed schedules, but it may be privately hired as well.

[4] Originating in Bologna and heading for Venice, the luxury Venice Simplon Orient Express has just left the Saint-Anton train station in Arlberg (Austria).
[5] The panoramic train is a special passenger train and is greatly beloved in the USA.
[6] The interior of the Pullman carriage of the luxury "Pullman Orient Express" train.

427

The name of the
"Trans-Siberian" train (Russia)
itself already evokes escape
and adventure.

For more than two hundred years, train journeys have evoked adventure, discovery and exoticism. With high-speed trains and airplanes, the 20th century has witnessed the reduction of distances in an incredible manner.

Curiously enough, dreams and romance remain the privileged domain of the train. This statement may be confirmed every day on railways running alongside the Nile, tackling the two great cordillera of the Andes, or on the lines crossing Europe, sweeping passengers along in magnificent palaces on rails. Who has never dreamt of meeting a "woman of the wagon-lit" or attempting the adventure of the "Trans-Siberian," a name evoking mythical journeys and exotic and colorful images? With or without the name, all of them allow the discovery of distant countries, a way to come to know them in their own rhythm, where the passing of time is often not the main preoccupation. Without any doubt, these "trains at the end of the world" remain the best way to discover such little-known regions and meet local people. Although the comfort in those places is a far cry from Western standards, the intensity of the journey can only bring surprise as the train, better than any other transport means, brings home the living reality of the local people.

Very few train can aspire to bring so many flavors and delights in this sense. Such as traversing Vietnam in ancient trains with wooden seats, crossing the Andes and encountering soroche or altitude sickness

Exotic Journeys

caused by the rarefied air, or the pleasant chattering of a steam train while giraffes roam at large in Africa.

[1] A "ferrobus," a sort of bus on rails, is running in Ecuador for a group of European tourists.
[2] The "Eastern and Oriental Express" train, intended for tourists of means, runs in Burma.
[3] "The Ghan," a genuine long-distance train in Australia, is equipped with gaming machines in a casino carriage and a library salon for the long journey.

[4] The "Canadian" train operated by VIA Rail provides for the Toronto-Vancouver connection.
[5] Departing from Cairo, this Egyptian passenger train composed of air-conditioned carriages is going to Luxor.
[6] Looking as though it has just escaped from a film, this train is running in Jordan on the very scenic line of Hedjaz.

[1] Colorful crowds around a passenger train on the Bolivian railway network.

[2] The train station atmosphere around a Moscow-Beijing train. Passengers on board this unit may sell or buy various products.

[3] The bridge on the River Kwai (Thailand) – the real one, which is very different from the one in the film – is visited by many tourists coming from all over the world.

[4] A dining coach of the "Trans-Siberian," a comfort train that has been little modernized, also remains a meeting place.
[5] A pleasant welcome in Argentina where a sign says "Have a nice journey!"
[6] In South Africa, this tourist train is both nostalgic and exotic.

[1] The beautiful exotic
atmosphere at Rufisque station
in Senegal.
[2] The private "Rocky
Mountaineer" train enables
the memorable exploration
of Rocheuses, Canada.
[Right] The Moroccan Railways
network offers tourists many
possibilities. The picture shows
a Casablanca-Marrakesh
express.

[1] The very colourful atmosphere of a train station visited during the journey of the "Chihuahua Al Pacifico" train in Mexico.
[2] A Paraguay steam train maintained and operated for tourists.
[3] In Australia, the "Kuranda Scenic Railway" attracts many tourists.

[4] The breakfast service on board a night train in South Africa.
[5] This train is running in the breathtaking scenerey of Patagonia (Argentina).
[6] The well-developed Indian railway network offers many possibilities for exploring.

МОСКВА-УЛАН-БАТОР

[1] A passenger train departing from the train station in Yerevan, the capital of Armenia.
[2] The itinerary plate of this Russian sleeping carriage indicates: Moscow to Ulaanbaatar (Mongolia).
[3] The South Korean network offers many possibilities for exploring this captivating Asian country.

[4] With the trains of the American Amtrak company, exploring the USA becomes much easier. Long journeys may be undertaken on board very comfortable night trains.
[5] China has a dense railway network at its disposal which makes it possible to fully experience this vast country.
[6] The passenger trains owned by the Canadian company VIA Rail connect the country's main cities.

Railway
Model-Building

Works of art on one hand, toys on the other, for centuries people have been manufacturing miniatures, lead soldiers, figurines, models of ships and so on. Therefore it is no surprise that railway model-making developed only a few years after the invention of railways.

These objects were the children's dream of that era. The intrusion into the country of a few dozen examples of steel "monsters" belching steam and smoke awakened their curiosity. The toy manufacturers quickly realized this windfall, and from the middle of the 19th century begin manufacturing numerous wooden replicas. Very soon they switched to more sophisticated constructions, sometimes in tin.

However, the toys were not the reduced models of today. One of the first train-toys appeared in Germany in 1866. It is a "floor-runner" driven by steam thanks to a boiler that generates steam from the heating of alcohol. It was not without its hazards.

Although railway modelling in metal has developed mostly in the O gauge since the 1950s, the plastic HO gauge, less space-intensive and less expensive, experienced a boom at the end of the 1960s. The multiplication of specialized companies diversified model production.

The models are presented to the public at display events that ensure their promotion.

A Passion for Model-Making

Other gauges appeared, with the goal of cornering new parts of the market. Whether sophisticated or plain, the model networks followed the basic idea: this is a hobby shared among friends in clubs or practised at home on one's one in a room adapted to that purpose. The dream often does the rest.

[1] A railcar and its trailer in a miniature network of the Railway Garden in Isère (France).

[2] The Madurodam Theme Park in the Netherlands offers a small railway network.

[3] The Swiss Vapeur Parc in Bouveret, Switzerland, is traversed by real miniature steam trains.

[4] A luxury train of the 1930s is reproduced at the N gauge.
[5] The diorama – a representation of a small scene – is a form of model-making at its best. Dismountable and transportable, the diorama can be shown in public.

[1] A crossing with gates: cars are waiting for the train to pass, just like in real life.

[2] The steam depot, a popular theme of railway model makers.

[3] An exhibition network made at the O gauge. This type is highly appreciated by visitors at public events and contributes to the promotion of rail enthusiasm.

[4] Model makers are real artists capable of constructing reproductions such as this magnificent steam locomotive.
[5] Certain model makers are also passionate collectors, who search for rare pieces prices can which can fetch very high prices.
[6] The O scale is sizeable and requires a certain amount of room to make lifelike demonstrations, as here at a public model-making exhibition.

[1] The networks are often thematic: this one is devoted to HO-gauge tramways.
[2] A beautiful small-scale reproduction of a "Pacific" North heading a reproduction of the "Flèche d'Or" train.
[3] The "Flèche d'Or" name used by the French Jep company fought a long battle for the hearts of model makers.

FLÈCHE D'OR
JeP

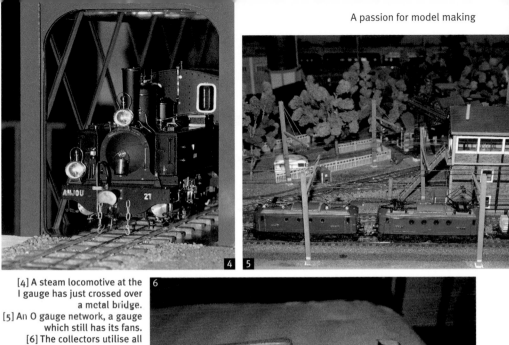

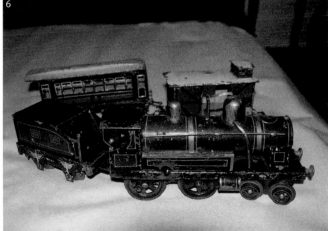

[4] A steam locomotive at the I gauge has just crossed over a metal bridge.
[5] An O gauge network, a gauge which still has its fans.
[6] The collectors utilise all available commercial channels to discover rare pieces like this old locomotive manufactured by the Jep company.

[1] This miniature reproduction of a locomotive of 1871 really runs on steam.

[2] These models may be modest but are not lacking in charm.
[3] A real miniature steam train carrying children in the Swiss Transport Museum in Lucerne during special days devoted to model railways.

[4] This diorama preserves the atmosphere of the 1950s with a SNCF railcar dawdling on a secondary line.
[5] More developed, this N gauge network is devoted to the French carriage rolling stock.

A s in the real railways, small-scale models also faced various problems with gauges and standards.

Standardisation was not at the forefront of their creators' interest either, and the systems encompassed an array of various gauges.

First of all, "I" gauge was created, with a gauge of 45 mm (1.8 in.) – it corresponds to the 1/32 scale in relation to the standard gauge of real trains; then the "O" came, with a 33 mm (1.30 in.) gauge for the 1/43.5 scale; later the "HO" (half zero) gauge appeared, with a 16.5 mm (0.64 in.) gauge for the 1/87 scale that is in most common use today. The 1/160, with a gauge of 9 mm (0.35 in.), the "TT" and even the "Z" at 1/220, Märklin's monopoly, were added a few years later. The same scales may also come in a variety of metric gauge forms, becoming thus "HOe", "Oe", etc. In the majority of developed countries, there are many brands: Märklin, Fleischmann, Tillig and Bemo in Germany; Hornby in Great Britain; Jep and Jouef in France; Rivarossi or Lima in Italy; Roco in Austria; Mehano in Slovenia; Bachmann in the USA. this industrial sector was not spared from market forces and these companies also experienced consolidations and takeovers: Hornby took over Lima, Rivarossi, Jouef and Bachmann as well, thus ensuring the production of Liliput. However, skilled craftsmen remain, and sometimes successfully offer rare models in limited series, even occasionally single models to those truly "crazy about railways." Among the most prestigious are the Swiss companies Fulgurex and Lemaco, which manufacture

A Question of Scale

true masterpieces in the "I", "O" and "HO" gauges. At the end of the 19th century, the catalogue of small-scale models was expanded so far that it is possible to reproduce period scenes with adequate equipment and all the necessary accessories.

[1] An HO presentation network of the German Märklin company.

[2] A beautiful network at the N gauge (1/160), presented by Minitrix.
[3] Manufactured at the O gauge, this E 94 appeared in a catalogue of the Fulgurex company in Switzerland.

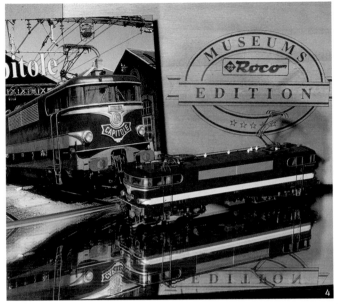

[4] To accompany the distribution of a limited BB 9200 edition in HO, the Austrian company Roco put out an exclusive piece of work devoted to the train "le Capitole."

[5] Until the reunification of Germany, the equipment manufactured in GDR bore the Piko brand. This brand still exists.

[6] This beautiful German S 3/6 was made at the O gauge by the Swiss Fulgurex company.

[1] A display cabinet of small-scale HO models, manufactured by the French Jouef company.
[2] In the USA, the Bachman company manufactures mainly American small-scale HO models.
[3] Fleischmann (Germany) made an 040 D of SNCF in HO.

[4] Presented in the network of a model maker, this SNCF CC 7100 in HO made by Rivarossi (Italy) has a proud bearing.
[5] A CC 7100 of SNCF was made in N by Minitrix (Germany).
[6] A Re 4/4 IV owned by CFF (Switzerland), manufactured in HO by Roco (Austria).

[1] This beautiful HOe scale (1/87) "Mallet" is manufactured by the Gécomodel company.

[2] The Italian company Lima presents its products in animated networks.
[3] The Swiss Lemaco company, another expert in the model-making world, manufactured this magnificent SNCF 150 C.

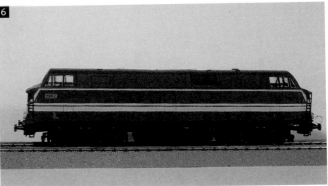

[4] Detail of a beautiful 103 series CC of manufactured by Roco in HO.
[5] At the time of public salons and public expositions, the German company Fleischmann showed its display networks at HO and N, both scales from their catalogue.
[6] A display of a Belgian locomotive in HO by Roco. The couplings are not shown.

[1] A sleeping carriage of the T2S type manufactured in N by Roco. This scale allows for the creation of beautiful compositions.
[2] A presentation of French small-scale models manufactured by Roco, with the X 2800 railcar in both the original version and in the "Massif central" version, painted in blue/gray.

[3] The electric HO m locomotive of the "Crocodile" type manufactured by the German Bemo company is running in the network of a Swiss train enthusiast.
[4] Another "Crocodile" locomotive, this time in HO, reproduces the ÖBB series CC 1020. This model, consequently improved, may be included in the Roco catalogue.

Index

The numbers in italics refer to the photo captions.

PHOTO CREDITS

The photographs in this book come from the Edelweiss Text and Picture Agency
(pictures taken by André Papazian, Michel Destombes, Thierry Favre, Pascal Letzelter, Camille Bruneau,
Serge der Mathéossian, Thierry Nicolas, Jean Tricoire, Daniel Ponroy and Olivier Werner).
Several photographs are from the private collection of the authors.

Grateful acknowledgements are offered to the associations, museums, and railway companies
who gave their consent to publish these photographs.

Main photograph on the cover: ©Georgina Bowater/Corbis
Other works in the 1001 PHOTOGRAPHS series:

HORSES
BABY ANIMALS
FOOTBALL
DOGS
AIRPLANES
CATS
DREAM CARS